The
EMOTIONAL
INTELLIGENCE
Workbook

Jill Dann and Derek Dann

We dedicate this workbook to all of our clients and associate practitioners, past and present, and to all who seek to apply the power of emotional intelligence as a route to greater fulfilment.

Jill Dann has survived in business since 1987, through several recessions, and has helped others during tough times and boom periods to hone a keen edge to get ahead of competitors, whether for a job, contract or university place. She has coached people of all ages and backgrounds – business, academic, scientific – from the UK, USA, Australasia, Europe and South America. She writes online every month for Ashridge Business School as well as undertaking change management roles for clients.

Following 20 years as a Royal Navy officer with staff and ship command experience, Derek Dann now applies his adapted military leadership skills to the whole spectrum of management from supervisory and junior levels to executive board members. He provides an integrated approach through coaching and mentoring, facilitation, learning and development and consulting to business performance acceleration at all levels, with particular emphasis on the differentiators of success within individuals, teams and organizations in the private and public sectors.

The EMOTIONAL INTELLIGENCE Workbook

Jill Dann and Derek Dann

Hodder Education

338 Euston Road, London NW1 3BH.

Hodder Education is an Hachette UK company

First published in UK 2012 by Hodder Education

First published in US 2012 by The McGraw-Hill Companies, Inc.

British Library Cataloguing in Publication Data: a catalogue record for this title is available from the British Library.

Library of Congress Catalog Card Number: on file.

10 9 8 7 6 5 4

The publisher has used its best endeavours to ensure that any website addresses referred to in this book are correct and active at the time of going to press. However, the publisher and the authors have no responsibility for the websites and can make no guarantee that a site will remain live or that the content will remain relevant, decent or appropriate.

The publisher has made every effort to mark as such all words which it believes to be trademarks. The publisher should also like to make it clear that the presence of a word in the book, whether marked or unmarked, in no way affects its legal status as a trademark.

Every reasonable effort has been made by the publisher to trace the copyright holders of material in this book. Any errors or omissions should be notified in writing to the publisher, who will endeavour to rectify the situation for any reprints and future editions.

Hachette UK's policy is to use papers that are natural, renewable and recyclable products and made from wood grown in sustainable forests. The logging and manufacturing processes are expected to conform to the environmental regulations of the country of origin.

www.hoddereducation.co.uk

Cover image © Vivid Pixels – Fotolia

Typeset by Cenveo Publisher Services.

Printed and bound by CPI Group (UK) Ltd, Croydon, CR0 4YY

Acknowledgement

We acknowledge the support of all friends and family, workmates and clients who have contributed so much to our deepening understanding of Emotional Intelligence over the past 14 years.

Their honesty, openness and trust in us have been both humbling and inspiring.

Contents

CONTENTS

How to use this workbook

The aim of this workbook is to give you a set of self-help techniques that you can experiment with and eventually master yourself.

Terms frequently used in this book are defined as follows:

Intelligence Quotient (IQ) is defined as 100 times the Mental Age (MA) divided by the Chronological Age (CA) – see References and resources for a definition of IQ and Binet's works.

Emotional Intelligence (EI) is one of a number of types of intelligence.

Emotional Intelligence Quotient (EQ) is a measure of Emotional Intelligence usually used in the context of intelligence quotient. EQ varies depending on the conceptual model used as the basis for measurement. Whereas our IQ is essentially a given, EQ can be nurtured in the home environment, developed in a corporate culture and worked on privately as an individual through self-directed learning (see Chapter 1). This workbook is designed mainly for the last of these.

Explicit knowledge is knowledge and expertise that is easy to express and to pass on to other people. Knowledge becomes wisdom when it has been put repeatedly to use, providing the holder with anecdotal evidence of reliability, such as the knowledge-holder acting to prevent a bad outcome.

Wisdom is the capacity to realize what is of value in life, for oneself and others, such as knowledge, understanding and technological know-how. Bertrand Russell defined it as 'the capacity to take account of all the important factors in a problem and to attach to each its due weight'.

Tacit wisdom is a valuable source of know-how which can be lost to an employing organization unless it intervenes and provides staff with ways of passing on each capability; for instance, tacit wisdom can be drawn out by specific interviewing techniques. Those with tacit wisdom are often seen as experts who need to be immersed in situations in order to access and express what outstanding capabilities they would demonstrate in such a scenario. Gained over time, this contextual expertise is not easy for one person to pass on to another. People find it difficult to verbalize and to structure the content; they do not consciously 'know what they know'.

→ An overview of emotional intelligence

The content and exercises in this workbook cover a broad range of emotional intelligence which can be studied further in the References and resources.

- ▶ Sociological (human interaction, inter and intra) – the way I manage myself, work with people, mix socially and relate to my community.
- ▶ Physiological (human mind/body linking functions) – the way I look after my health using positive emotions and working with the mind/body link.
- ▶ Psychological (human mind) – my ability to predict my performance, to identify triggers and to manage the outcome, breaking unhelpful patterns from the past.

The following definitions further explain the steps in the cycle illustrated in the diagram below.

1 **Self-aware** – Having an awareness of feelings, an ability to recognize one's emotions, the intensity of each feeling, the effects of them and an ability to deal with emotional outcomes.

2 **Self-controlled** – Being self-regulating, managing emotions and holding back unhelpful impulses. It involves knowing, understanding and accepting our strengths and weaknesses.

3 **Aware of others** – Able to recognize the intensity and nature of emotions experienced by others, able to constantly pick up emotional cues, knowing what is being felt and thought, even when it is not explicitly said. People with this competence can adjust their behaviour according to emotional cues to achieve rapport, aiding the quality of communication. They can appreciate not only what a person is saying, but also why they are saying it.

4 **Manages relationships** – Having achieved strengths in the previous capabilities, individuals can put these all together to inspire others, to help develop other people, to act as a change catalyst and to be a major influencer with organizational and political awareness.

5 **Has high EQ** – the development cycle is not at an end at this point; there is the opportunity for further renewal of capability if you have an appetite to succeed and to progress further. When you have a high EQ you are adept at interpreting the emotional roots of your own thinking and behaviour, thus *choosing* your actions to influence outcomes. You are also capable of good insights into the behaviour of others.

The cyclical nature of development is reflected in the diagram below and others in this opening section. The workbook structure mirrors this progressive process of developing higher emotional intelligence. The cycle is unending as challenges crop up through everyday life and these inspire you to progress further.

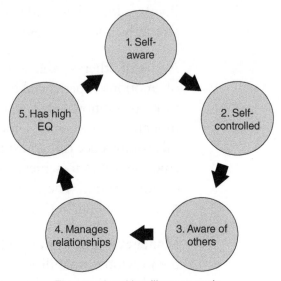

The emotional intelligence cycle

The following model for this workbook shows how self-awareness is the first building block for all the other areas. By developing this capability, it also becomes possible to be more self-controlled and aware of others. However, you cannot be self-controlled effectively without being self-aware.

By having better self-control, you can have a clearer head to focus on other people and identify the emotions that they may be feeling. This way your head is not busy and muddled so your attention can turn outwards. These first three capabilities then equip you to tackle the more advanced capabilities required to manage relationships powerfully and effectively.

	Individual	Others
Identification	**1. Self-aware** Have an awareness of feelings, an ability to recognize one's emotions, the intensity of each feeling, the effects of them and an ability to deal with emotional outcomes.	**3. Aware of others** Recognize the intensity and nature of others' emotional cues, can adjust their behaviour accordingly to achieve rapport, aiding communication quality. They appreciate both what is said and why it's said.
Direction	**2. Self-controlled** Be self-regulating, managing emotions and holding back unhelpful impulses. It involves knowing, understanding and accepting our strengths and weaknesses.	**4. Manages relationships** Have achieved strengths in the previous capabilities, individuals can put these all together to inspire others, to help develop other people, to act as a change catalyst and to be a major influencer having organizational and political awareness.

The scope of emotional intelligence

My emotional intelligence

Read the description in each of the quadrants which scopes emotional intelligence as defined in the chart above. Record your instant gut feelings and thoughts as you read each description.

→ Self-aware – what are my strengths?

_____

_____

_____

_____

→ Self-aware – what are my learning gaps?

_____

_____

_____

_____

Self-controlled – what are my strengths?

_____

_____

_____

_____

→ Self-controlled – what are my learning gaps?

_____

_____

_____

_____

→ Aware of others – what are my strengths?

_____

_____

_____

_____

→ Aware of others – what are my learning gaps?

_____

_____

_____

_____

→ Manages relationships – what are my strengths?

_____

_____

_____

_____

→ Manages relationships – what are my learning gaps?

_____

_____

_____

_____

Life as we know it

Which of the following do you feel applies to you? Tick all that apply.

The modern world makes a lot of demands on us:

▶ to be able to be effective when away from the office as well as being effective in the workplace

- ► to be able to win co-operation from people who are not subordinate in any way. This can be from, say, running a highly productive meeting to agreeing a new budget or the design of an extension at home
- ► to create a climate where we can be honest, to tell the truth even when it's painful to the one who needs to hear it. To have the resilience to see such things through to completion
- ► to recognize and effectively deal with the unmet emotional needs of ourselves, our family, partners, friends and colleagues
- ► to deal with thwarted expectations, plans and ambitions as the world becomes more globalized and competitors impede rivals' new strategies, products and services.

Most of us are 'time poor' and fewer of us are 'cash rich' these days so we want something that we can control ourselves and which saves us time once it's working for us. Classically, people want to control their own development with sufficient information to manage learning and progress. Typical issues are coping skills around work/life balance, stress management, and relationships with spouse/partner, siblings, children, parents, bosses, colleagues, customers and suppliers. In addition, most of us seek to learn because we want to get more out of life, to feel more energized and less anxious.

What are the typical issues that come up in everyday life for you? Make notes here.

_____

_____

_____

_____

You may observe unhelpful behaviour in others before you see it in your own behaviour; adults see it in their children or in elderly parents who grow to be more reliant on them. Most of us recall awkward moments when we have lost control or experienced misunderstandings with others. It is indeed a common human experience. Whether the situation is an upset with teenagers, a work colleague or an elderly relative or neighbour, it takes more time to clear up than you can afford to spend. It also leaves a bitter and lingering taste in your mouth.

Make notes here of what you see other people do or say which is unhelpful.

_____

_____

_____

_____

_____

_____

_____

_____

You may feel comfortable with many of your characteristics and less happy with others. To self-manage effectively, as well as knowing your goals and guiding values, you need to be aware of optimum stress levels and the ways in which you cope. You should expect to feel better mentally and physically after raising your EQ but it would also be perfectly normal to have lapses back to some unhelpful behaviour. However, you would have better personal insight about why the lapse occurred and be able to prevent a recurrence.

Make notes here of previous persistent 'bad habits' which you have attempted to tackle.

_____

_____

_____

_____

_____

_____

_____

→ The workbook programme

To become more mature and to be authentic in the company of others, we each have to connect with our inner selves and our manifested uniqueness. Use this workbook to develop a higher emotional intelligence than you have currently. Each chapter has a test to identify where you are. You will need to identify your goals and the reasons why you want to do this.

► I want to use the workbook to understand where I have difficulties now in understanding my feelings, especially where this leads to behaviour which I later regret.

► I will identify how much time I waste now by not getting things straight, right first time or in harmony with others.

► In practical everyday ways, I will use the workbook to develop a deeper appreciation of how my brain works in order to take advantage of its design, e.g. to overcome phobias, improve memory or to have greater awareness of others.

▶ I want to use the workbook to guide me from an inner core of learned self-awareness to developing better control and insightful prediction of difficulties, allowing me to plan for better emotional outcomes in relationships, whether professional, familial or personal.

Thus, the outcomes of successfully progressing through the workbook help with your need:

▶ to have self-knowledge encompassing an accurate self-identity, so that how most other people see you is approximate to your own self-image

▶ to learn to have sufficient humility to accept feedback, both positive and negative, and to act on it appropriately

▶ to become aware if your *stated* values are compromised by your *actual* behaviour. For example, most people think themselves honest, yet are capable of telling 'little white lies' for reasons that feel justified.

While there are many other models of emotional intelligence, any model of emotional intelligence will need you to do or seek to have:

▶ the spark of self-awareness at a level to seek self-knowledge and insights

▶ a desire for emotional literacy so that you can name the emotions as you experience them and identify their intensity; for instance, there is a difference between being mildly irritated and absolutely furious with someone, but the emotion felt is still anger

▶ a need to tame the 'internal observer' in order to increase self-control, so your inner voice is under your control and is helpful, not interrupting your thoughts and distracting you

▶ an acceptance of intelligences other than just intellectual IQ

▶ a need to increase understanding of and competence in using the mind/body link, recognizing that head, heart and gut collectively need to be observed and managed, e.g. inappropriate stress reactions.

Therefore, to develop what is outwardly evident to others as highly emotionally intelligent behaviour, you need to start by igniting your inner core of awareness as illustrated in the diagram below. Start from the inside and work outwards.

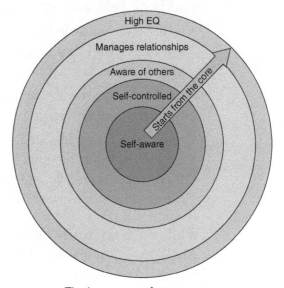

The inner core of awareness

Essentially, you need to understand your place in the world and to be happy with it.

The differences that you and others will notice are typically:

▶ you are in charge of your habits instead of bad habits being in charge of you

▶ you appear less anxious and seem calm even if others are expressing strong emotions around you

▶ you will have more time for pleasurable and productive things, replacing time spent clearing up confusion or making apologies

▶ people see that you recognize when a situation is going sour

▶ you plan the outcome of a regular meeting proactively and organize accordingly to get a better result

- you become highly effective at work, staving off conflict and spotting hidden agendas
- you organize a better holiday or day trip for the family
- you are more able to cope with change and to catalyse change in others
- other people enjoy working with you and request you to work on their projects and initiatives.

Part of undertaking the exercises in the early chapters is to identify how this workbook will affect your life and bring you greater success. Each of the chapters will:
- have a definition of the emotional intelligence competence and a set of questions for self-assessment of the reader's current place on the scale or for peer review
- have a number of exercises made up of questionnaires/ assessments, checklists, workplace or home exercises, 'rehearsals' practising particular competencies, and others
- end with any update of your personal development plan (PDP) required after the other exercises for the chapter are completed
- be cross-related to other chapters as required and set in context.

Summary

The chapter structure follows the flow suggested from becoming self-aware, to being self-controlled, then able to be more aware of others and able to manage relationships.

The types of exercises that will be used are mostly sets of questions for you to ponder and reflect on (short questionnaires). The reason for this is that emotional intelligence is not about the acquisition of knowledge. It is much less tangible in nature. However, if you have experienced being with someone who is using high emotional intelligence then you are generally aware of it. High EQ people tend to have an impact on others which leaves an impression; you are likely to feel challenged, supported and inspired by them.

Some specific competencies are selected for their own chapter within the four domains; self-motivation falls within the domain of self-control, but since it is an important competence for a self-directed programme it is given its own chapter and exercises.

The brain science that has emerged over the last ten years has been similarly brought into focus for those who are interested, although Chapter 2 can be skimmed or skipped by those with a different focus.

The last four chapters are elements from the relationship management domain: conflict resolution, achievement orientation, organizational awareness, and teamwork and collaboration. As we make our way in the world, these are useful for those undertaking any self-directed study involving experimenting and reflecting on learning experiences.

Therefore, the flow of learning looks like this:

Understand how to use this workbook
↓
Have mastered self-directed learning
↓
Are taking advantage of brain design
↓
Have mastered your self-awareness
↓
Have mastered your self-control
↓
Develop your self-motivation
↓
Develop your awareness of others
↓
Develop your management of others
↓
Become more resilient
↓
Develop your influence skills
↓
Have mastered conflict resolution
↓
Understand achievement orientation
↓
Understand organizational awareness
↓
Understand teamwork and collaboration
↓
Have higher EQ and want to progress further

In addition to the exercises in each chapter, at the back of the workbook there is a References and resources section pointing you to further sources of information or tools for that topic, such as assessments, toolkits, books, e-books, audio and relevant films which aid learning on the competency.

1 self-directed learning

In its broadest meaning, 'self-directed learning' describes a process 'in which individuals take the initiative, with or without the help of others, in diagnosing their learning needs, formulating learning goals, identifying human and material resources for learning, choosing and implementing appropriate learning strategies, and evaluating learning outcomes'. (Knowles, 1975).

WHAT IT IS

An example of self-directed learning is the undertaking of a targeted programme of study with defined milestones which involve development of a study plan and assessments of progress leading to defined outcomes or goals. The creation of the self-directed study plan often involves diagnostic exercises, usually open questions to cause the learner to reflect on where they are now, and the results of the exercises help shape the plan. The objective is to conclude where the learner wants to be, by when, in terms of improvements to their behaviour, knowledge and skills.

Self-directed learning

Nowadays, the resources and references available to individuals in the home environment are many: examples are integrated internet television provided via cable, satellite or terrestrial television, and unified communications integrating a laptop, PC or tablet with mobile phone applications. Public and academic libraries also remain valuable sources for the learner. Thus, this approach will appeal to those for whom a self-designed, self-directed strategy and programme of learning is attractive.

→ Understanding motivation and why adults learn

Acquiring a higher EQ through this developmental process may be different to your education, training and development experiences prior to this.

▶ Adults learn because they want to learn; adults are not in compulsory education.

▶ Adults acquire experience through everyday occurrences, both good and bad.

▶ In organizations, adults will learn whether the company directs it or not; individuals will adapt to progress, survive and compete.

Because of the nature of emotional intelligence, in what way is developing it different? Emotional intelligence is most effectively developed through experiential learning, i.e. learning through experiences of the senses. Experiential learning has more impact since people connect emotionally, often without even knowing or naming what they feel. By engaging in a meaningful experience, something is more likely to shift in our amygdala (see Chapter 2) and this opens us to changing our behavioural patterns.

The most appropriate definition of experiential learning for the purposes of emotional intelligence is 'education that occurs as a direct participation in the events of life' (Houle, 1980). Here, learning is sponsored by people themselves, not by some formal educational institution. Learning is achieved through reflection upon everyday experiences; most adults learn this way. This can be reinforced through linguistic communication – talking therapies, sharing learning with others or through coaching and mentoring.

→ What's important

It is critical in self-directed learning to:
▶ experiment and practise. This way may stretch most adults to become more flexible in using a variety of learning styles to a preferred style (Smith, 2001)
▶ develop and use relationships as part of your learning and change process
▶ identify and work with good role models (see later exercise). Reflect with them regarding their own perception and experience of managing personal change in the past

- ▶ generate settings where you feel psychologically safe to experiment and practise
- ▶ reflect on assessment results with regard to your learning style
- ▶ reflect on past examples of great learning experiences and prior pitfalls. Identify what was memorable and what sustained you
- ▶ recognize that the process is adaptive and evolutionary; a focus on overcoming gaps with a sense of deficit or loss is less effective than using strengths to overcome issues.

Consider what would be most helpful to you during this type of development.

Foundation exercises

These exercises continue to introduce the following 12 chapters, including how each of them fits together into a cohesive whole.

Who do I want to be? If you have a clear set of goals or objectives in mind then document them now. Otherwise, complete this as insights emerge from doing the other exercises.

_____

_____

_____

_____

_____

_____

Who am I now?

_____

_____

_____

_____

_____

What are my strengths?

_____

_____

_____

_____

_____

What are my learning gaps?

_____

_____

_____

_____

_____

_____

How am I doing with my learning?

_____

_____

_____

_____

_____

_____

_____

Have I go there yet? (milestone check)

_____

_____

_____

_____

_____

_____

_____

→ The learning ladder

Achieving goals leads to an emotional high but the process of getting on top of a subject or skill involves earlier steps which, however fleetingly, involve discomfort or frustration.

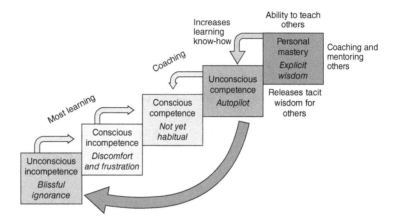

The learning ladder

When you are on the first rung of the learning ladder, you are in blissful ignorance of what you do not know. As you learn more and are impacted more, you learn how lacking in skill or knowledge you were. If you progress to mastering the subject, you become conscious of your new capability. As a matter of routine you may not perform competently; it is not yet habitual. By the fourth step you will know it so well, you do not even have to think about it; you are on autopilot.

▶ Unconscious incompetence – you do not know what you do not know.

▶ Conscious incompetence – you now know what you do not know.

▶ Conscious competence – you know what you know but have to think about it.

▶ Unconscious competence – you feel as if you have always been proficient.

► Personal mastery – you learn to articulate and extrapolate ideas to teach others.

At this level, you can help others acquire knowledge and good practice and learn how to capitalize on it. You can learn to coach, mentor and teach others easily and in context.

My past learning experiences

Reflect on past examples of great learning experiences and prior pitfalls. Describe them briefly.

_____

_____

_____

_____

_____

_____

_____

_____

Identify what was memorable.

_____

_____

_____

_____

_____

_____

Explain what sustained you.

_____

_____

_____

_____

_____

_____

_____

_____

_____

Describe a learning experience where you felt awkward or uncomfortable. On which step of the learning process were you?

_____

_____

_____

_____

_____

_____

_____

_____

Identify an instance of being aware of doing something new which you have not had much experience of. What did it feel like?

_____

_____

_____

_____

_____

_____

_____

Identify times when you seem to be on autopilot. How much experience have you got and what training was involved, if any?

_____

_____

_____

_____

_____

_____

_____

Identify any instance of you being treated as the expert in something. What did it feel like?

_____

_____

_____

_____

_____

_____

_____

_____

_____

_____

_____

_____

→ The route to personal mastery

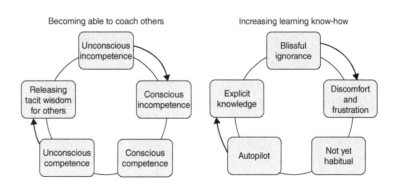

'Learning is the most important of all human capabilities and will never become obsolete. Continuous learning is the key to innovation and competitiveness.'

Dr Peter Honey

MAKING IT HAPPEN – ACCEPTING SUPPORT

Not all of us are predisposed to share our learning processes, especially when it is emotional learning. However, having someone to 'challenge and support, in equal measure' can be pivotal to success. Making our commitments public significantly increases our chances of completing them; 'go it alone' individuals usually fail to progress through their list of action items. The reality is that it is rare for a plan to be finished before circumstances have changed, creating a state of flux. However, fluctuations are normal and learning to adapt is part of becoming an adult.

If you have any experience of trying to consolidate and embed learning in isolation, then please accept the strong recommendation that you seek support by sharing your plan with a trusted individual. Choose an appropriately interested person who will be supportive of your action plan to draw on for empathy and support, preferably one with the expertise to act as a mentor. You may wish to have one supporter in your work environment and another in your personal life. They must be reliable people, the sort of person on whom you could call when faced with an emotional emergency.

Briefing a buddy

Use the following exercise to think out how you would brief possible learning 'buddies'. If you talk matters out with them over the phone, make a note of the conversation so that you can compare notes. Remember that if you feel challenged, this may be healthy for you.

Possible learning buddies would need to understand the following.

Your expectations of them

_____

_____

_____

_____

The scope and scale of the undertaking

_____

_____

_____

_____

How stretching it will be

_____

_____

_____

_____

The challenges you are likely to face

_____

_____

_____

The outcomes you are seeking

_____

_____

_____

_____

The timescales that you wish to achieve

_____

_____

_____

_____

Seek feedback on the draft of your plan, and as you progress through the period of your planned development. Make notes here.

_____

_____

THE PERSONAL DEVELOPMENT PLAN

A personal development plan (PDP) is a simple approach to tracking and setting targets, and a tried and tested one. Milestones used to check progress were mentioned earlier in the chapter. It is best to keep things simple so that you keep your records up to date. Put this simple table on your mobile phone, tablet or another device which you keep readily to hand and which links to your calendar, so that activities can be scheduled and reminders/alerts set. You can grab moments to review your learning at many points in a busy week, e.g. while commuting, having a coffee or waiting for your favourite television programme to start or download.

Set your own list and get feedback on the things that you need to start doing, stop doing, do more or do less.

Example of a partly completed PDP	
I will start ...	*I will do more ...*
I will stop ...	*I will do less ...*

Grade your current level of competence on a scale of 1–5 and then define the target level that you would like to achieve. Write these figures alongside the brief description of your actions

5 = Expert – practising at a level of excellence with a high degree of skill and vast knowledge base.

4 = Practitioner – proficient and above the minimum standard required due to experience and advanced knowledge.

3 = Foundation – meets the minimum standard of competence, familiar with and able to use relevant knowledge and skill.

2 = Basic – some or little knowledge/skill, but unable to practise at a competent level.

1 = Novice no knowledge/skill; requires extensive training.

In order to enjoy the fullness of what life has to offer, it is necessary to answer some hard questions about who you are. Time spent focusing on these things will help clarify what you want out of life. Traditionally, we just think of things we need to start doing or do better – good habits and practices. However, it is often the case that we are unaware of things which others know about us; things we should stop doing or do less of. It is a big step to ask someone to help in your development, but the benefits of acting on feedback are amazing once you steel yourself to do it. Have courage and start collecting items for your personal development plan.

The following completed personal development plan gives examples of the type of things that need attention. The plan needs to be graded item by item so that current capability and desired target are understood; preferably it should be agreed with your learning buddy.

Example of a completed PDP	
I will start . . . *1 To reflect on my performance weekly* *2 To seek feedback and act on it* *3 To practise challenging and supporting clients* *4 Being more self-confident and have a positive outlook*	*I will do more . . .* *1 Active listening* *2 Checking and summarizing* *3 Tolerating ambiguity to explore issues* *4 Disclosure to elicit issues with clients*
I will stop . . . *1 Interrupting people* *2 Waiting to jump in and not listening* *3 Overwhelming people with my knowledge* *4 Avoiding conflict and learn to resolve it collaboratively*	*I will do less . . .* *1 Admonishing myself for perceived failures* *2 Blaming others and being judgemental* *3 Making light of my success* *4 Making me the lowest priority*

Look through the list and you will see that items 1–3 of 'I will start' can be allocated a date straight away in your calendar, diary or schedule. The other benefit from you reflecting on your current commitments and interactions with others is to see opportunities which may arise for you to rehearse your improved emotional intelligence. The 'I will stop' actions can be practised socially and at home if you are anxious about trying the changed behaviour at work.

Create a folder on paper or on a computer and start to develop your learning agenda.

My learning agenda

My personal development plan needs to consider:

→ In what way are my ideal and real selves similar?

_____

_____

_____

_____

_____

_____

_____

→ In what way are my ideal and real selves different?

_____

_____

_____

_____

_____

_____

_____

_____

→ What would be the impact of developing better emotional intelligence? On home and life (community, social, hobbies)

_____

_____

_____

_____

_____

_____

_____

Make sure that your targets (goals) are C-SMART:

1 Challenging – they need to stretch you, and be challenging but not overly so.
2 Specific – they should be precisely defined.
3 Measurable – how will you know you have achieved them?
4 Achievable – it is demotivating to set targets or goals that are unachievable.
5 Relevant – make sure they are relevant to what you want to achieve.
6 Time-based – you must define a timescale within which you want to achieve them. Then you must revisit the plan to ensure you remain on track.

Role model

Think of a role model, someone you admire or have admired in the past.

→ Which characteristics did you admire in that person?

_____

_____

_____

_____

_____

_____

_____

→ Which characteristics do you see in yourself that you've admired in that person?

_____

_____

_____

_____

_____

_____

_____

→ Which of the identified characteristics do you want to adopt?

_____

_____

_____

_____

_____

_____

_____

→ What did they do that led you to recognize that you have new behaviours which you need to start doing, or do more of?

_____

_____

_____

_____

_____

_____

_____

→ What did a bad role model do that led you to recognize that you have old behaviours which you need to stop doing, or do less of?

_____

_____

_____

_____

_____

_____

_____

_____

Visualization

This technique is a physical and mental exercise using the imagination. Use it for many things, such as imagining yourself as your ideal self in the future. Use it to look back on your life and to guide you in setting goals and checking progress.

→ Visualize a line on the floor. Mark it with sticky notes.

→ Close your eyes and create a vision of your successful self at a future point in your life when you have achieved a goal.

→ Walk along the imaginary line to the point where you are a short time beyond achieving the milestone.

→ Imagine what your emotions are – what you can see, hear, smell and feel in your gut in response to what is going on around you.

→ Is anyone else there?

→ What can you see them doing or hear them saying?

→ How do you feel when you see and hear this?

→ Make the visualization as rich and colourful as possible, and in your imagination move around in three dimensions within it.

→ Record everything you have creatively visualized as if you were a camera, recording images as well as sounds.

→ On the spot, turn yourself around to face back towards the point where you started.

→ Bring on the rich visualization again until you are filled up with it.

→ What advice can you give your real self about reaching your goal at the milestone point visualized earlier?

→ How was the goal achieved?

→ What action was taken, and issues raised and overcome?

→ If you met a perceived barrier, what was it?

→ Concentrate on all of the learning experience about the barrier, such as discoveries of self-awareness and self-control.

→ If you are working with someone else and not alone, ask your observer to tell you about your body language while carrying out the exercise and any other observations.

→ What traits do you display as your ideal self?

→ What is your dominant motive for achievement? Why do you want to learn? This is your Personal Learning Agenda.

→ What goal(s) have you achieved at that desired future milestone as your ideal self?

→ When you got back to the end of the timeline, to the 'here and now', did you still want to achieve it?

→ What have you learned about your real self through this process?

→ What resources did you gather along the timeline, for example, courage, motivation?

Summary

The References and resources section covers an array of useful additional material and expert guidance to inspire you to design your own emotional intelligence study plan and to reinforce the content of each chapter. Some recommendations are:

► Learning relationships with others – if you want to get ahead, get a learning buddy.

► If you can afford it, get a skilled coach.

► Use your influencing skills to enrol others into making changes happen (see Chapter 9).

► Do seek feedback and act on it.

2 Taking advantage of your brain design

Emotional intelligence quotient (EQ) is frequently mentioned as the differentiator that makes people stand out from the crowd, yet it is not a cognitive skill like IT skills. There are some fast-track methods to raising EQ which may appear unusual. This chapter covers the outline findings, and further evidence is given in the Reference and resources section.

WHAT IT IS

Emotional intelligence is more about your way of *being* than of doing. The distinction can be clarified as being between:

▶ cognitive learning, which is about absorbing new data and insights into existing frameworks of association and understanding, such as in conventional education.

▶ emotional learning, which involves being authentic and in tune with your identity, values and beliefs. Skills associated with emotional intelligence develop throughout life. Changing habits, such as learning to listen more carefully or to give feedback skilfully and with the right attitude, is much more challenging than simply adding new information to old. If you are asked to get a new mobile app for teamwork, you will probably embrace the idea because it appeals. However, if you are told that you need to improve your ability to work productively with others, you are likely to be upset or offended, generating resistance to change.

▷ At the end of a lecture on emotional intelligence, do you think that anyone has a higher EQ? No, it is unlikely, as this is not experiential learning.

▷ At the end of completing assignments on the university intranet consisting of 20 emotional intelligence exercises, would students have a higher EQ? Potentially yes, if they made use of the material, but unless the assignments counted towards the course grade, the take-up of this type of enrichment material might be low.

▷ At the end of a degree course, graduates need to fit into the culture of their employer's company to be a good employee. If they are incentivized to adopt more emotionally intelligent behaviour through enrichment activities or marked assignments, this should equip them to be more successful in their first role.

→ Why brain design is important

Having a positive attitude and some emotional engagement is pivotal to success. There are a number of factors that increase your chances of attaining your goals:

▶ learning relationships
▶ learning environment
▶ memory, recall and emotions
▶ our memory during and after training or study
▶ experimenting and taking risks.

LEARNING RELATIONSHIPS

Taking a 'learning buddy', or trusted adviser, is strongly recommended. The relationship should be characterized by trust, a sense of security and mutual respect. It is wise to be challenged in designing and implementing your study plan.

Selecting my buddy

Who do I know who may be willing to support me in this development programme? Make notes here.

_____

_____

_____

_____

_____

_____

_____

Who do I know who has an undesired effect on emotional outcomes when we meet?

_____

_____

_____

_____

_____

_____

Can I recognize what they do that I respond to (a trigger behaviour)?

_____

_____

_____

_____

· ·

When we trust someone, we tend to have a rapport with them, physiologically experiencing appreciation and empathy. This visceral and mental response calms our pulse rate, blood pressure and brain-wave pattern. Blood flow to the brain is enhanced and a hormone release increases the amount of glucose going to the brain (brain food) aiding cognition and the laying down of memories (in order to recall learning later).

If we do not trust someone, however, subliminally we feel threatened by them and this invokes our fight, flight or freeze response. The limbic system (or emotional brain centre) evolved to deal with instinctive behaviours, such as eating, drinking, mating, defending ourselves and surviving. A part of the brain called the amygdala triggers this physiological response, thinking only in stark, survival-type choices:

▶ fight – will I win against this specific threat?

▶ flight – am I faster than it is?

▶ freeze – if I do not respond, will it stop seeing me as prey?

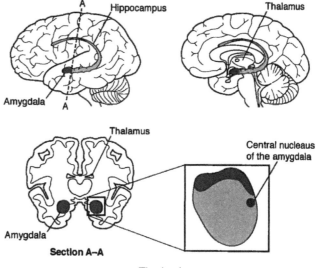

The brain

The amygdala consists of two almond-shaped structures in the limbic region. It promotes survival by continually scanning the environment and interpreting each new stimulus using multiple-sensory inputs of potential dangers in terms of whether it is safe or suspect. In colloquial terms, the amygdala asks:

▶ can I approach this or not?

▶ can I eat this or will it eat me?

▶ will I fight and win, or should I flee?

▶ if I freeze, will it leave me alone or not see me in the undergrowth?

The reason why we do not remember traumas experienced very early in life is explained by the parallel operation of our **explicit** (hippocampal) and **implicit** (amygdalic) memory systems. We are born with inbuilt templates, mental patterns for which we seek fulfilment in our environment. An example of this is the way a newborn baby instinctively seeks the nipple. Such innate patterns are necessarily incomplete, to encourage the flexibility needed to survive by adapting to changes in the environment. Thus, a newborn baby will accept a rubber teat simulating a mother's nipple.

We perceive the outside world through partially completed inner templates. Only the incoming stimuli which complete one of these pre-existing templates can be perceived. Stimuli that do not complete this pattern-matching process are not perceived.

If emotional arousal is sufficiently strong, it overrides the thinking brain altogether in order to obey the innate instinct to survive. Emotions operate from a good/bad, either/or perspective, such that it has been said, 'High emotional arousal makes us stupid'.

My phobias

Do you have any phobias which are inexplicable to you? Make notes here.

_____

_____

_____

_____

_____

_____

_____

Do you have an older relative, one who knew your parents and you as a child, who may be able to explain why you have this fear?

_____

_____

_____

Can you recognize the onset of the fear or do you avoid situations in which it may be triggered?

_____

_____

_____

_____

_____

All of a human's physical states from three months after conception until the age of five years are stored in the amygdala, together with the perceptual contexts which accompanied the physical states. In infancy, the amygdala is already able to record unconscious memories, although the hippocampus is still too immature. The amygdala performs two processes.

1 It stores any novel physical state with its associated perceptual context.

2 It retriggers the associated physical state when presented with a familiar perceptual context during a later episode.

At the age of about five years, the amygdala ends the first process but it continues the second, retriggering process for the remainder of a person's life. For example, if a pregnant mother slips and becomes frightened, her physiological state (which would comprise well-known defence reactions, such as a pounding heart, muscle tension, inhibition, flight, preparation for defensive attack) is experienced by the unborn baby in her womb.

The fright and associated physical states are stored in the baby's amygdala, along with the perceptual context of the falling motion. Regardless of whether the baby's mother experiences it, the baby may experience the same 'fright' retriggered by a subsequent slip through its associative learning of conditioned fear. Therefore, early childhood traumas can disturb the mental, physiological and behavioural functioning of adults by mechanisms that they cannot access consciously.

The same symptoms may be experienced 30 or 40 years later if the original falling motion in the prenatal slip is mimicked by turbulence during a plane flight. However, this similar perceptual context and the accompanying physical state experienced may now be associated consciously as a fear of flying. The original laying down of the memory of a falling motion and the associated fright is subconscious.

The amygdala appears to use the intense recollection of emotional memories in decoding feelings. Because it may trigger the 'fight or flight' syndrome, there is substantial evidence to suggest that learning can be prohibited by negative types of stress, in which glucose goes to the muscles while the blood flow to the brain becomes restricted. It may take an unhelpful length of time for the body to recover once stress or fright develops, making it difficult to breathe normally, to learn and to perform tasks at work.

However, the limbic system developed a rudimentary ability for memory and learning, to avoid going on full alert each time the senses detected a source of danger. It needed to be able to recognize which stimuli are threats and which are not, a process that we term 'pattern matching' and which still underlies our mental functioning today.

While humans need this adrenaline-fuelled defence mechanism in life-threatening circumstances, it can be counter-productive in everyday situations, as all thoughts and perceptions are preceded by emotions out of conscious awareness. Our capacity to discern finer detail is unavailable.

Tackling my phobias

If you want to tackle any of these phobias, makes notes about your intent.

_____

_____

_____

_____

_____

_____

Identify sources of support in tackling them.

_____

_____

_____

_____

_____

_____

Many other structures housed in the limbic system, and developed some millions of years before the neocortex, also help to encode our long-term memoriesed. This final part is the highest-order brain centre, concerned with thinking, planning, memory and other functions. While the limbic system is concerned with raw emotion, the higher centres put a more delicate spin on things, for instance, enlarging pleasure and desire into a capacity to bond with and care for other human beings.

That is why a non-threatening learning buddy is recommended, as creating trust, a sense of security and an atmosphere of mutual respect is conducive to learning and transferring what is learned to the long-term memory.

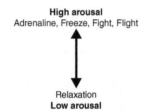

High arousal
Adrenaline, Freeze, Fight, Flight

Relaxation
Low arousal

The physiology of performance: the body's short-term system.
Based on Henry and Stephens, *Stress, health and the social environment*

THE LEARNING ENVIRONMENT

Your learning environment requires 'challenge and support in equal measure' from people, as well as good 'hygiene' factors to minimize distractions and physical discomfort, and so create an atmosphere conducive to achievement. If we are generally positive, the chemical dehydroepiandrosterone (DHEA), colloquially known as the 'happiness hormone', makes us feel good about ourselves and has a positive effect on our physiology.

Getting a sense of achievement when learning and celebrating attainment leads to the release of DHEA. If we are prone to think negatively, then the hormone cortisol cuts in to attempt to shift the balance towards a more positive outlook. The long-term effects of unbalanced amounts of cortisol combined with adrenaline on our general health are known to be detrimental.

The physiology of performance: the body's long-term system.
Based on Henry and Stephens, *Stress, health and the social environment*

However, cortisol, which is secreted by the adrenal glands, is an important hormone in the body. It is involved in the following functions, allowing the body to handle stress and to maintain the immune system:

▶ insulin release for blood sugar maintenance

▶ glucose metabolism feeding the brain and body

▶ immune function

▶ regulation of blood pressure

▶ inflammatory response.

When the body properly produces and uses cortisol, a person remains more alert and energized than when the adrenal glands experience complications such as adrenal fatigue. While cortisol is an important and helpful part of the body's response to stress, it is important for the body's relaxation response to be activated so the body's functions can return to normal following a stressful event. Stress hormones can reside in the body at high levels for several days, depending on the severity of the response to the perceived situation.

Because of today's high-stress culture, the body's stress response is activated so often that it does not always have a chance to return to normal, resulting in a state of chronic stress. Small increases in cortisol in the bloodstream have some positive effects:

▶ an energy burst for survival

▶ lower sensitivity to pain

- heightened memory functions
- maintaining homeostasis in the body
- a burst of increased immunity
- helping avoid extended emotional highs.

The physiology of performance: a lethal cocktail.
Based on Henry and Stephens, *Stress, health and the social environment*

Higher and more prolonged levels of cortisol with adrenaline in the bloodstream have long-term negative effects:

- impaired cognitive performance
- suppressed thyroid function
- blood sugar imbalances such as hyperglycaemia
- decreased bone density
- decrease in muscle tissue
- higher blood pressure
- lowered immunity, inflammatory responses in the body, slower wound healing, and other health consequences
- increased abdominal fat, associated with heart attacks, strokes, higher levels of 'bad' cholesterol (LDL) than 'good' cholesterol (HDL), which can lead to other health problems.

Stopping the *inappropriate* triggering of the survival system needs to be the focus of our development of stress management strategies and self-control in later chapters.

My triggers

Identify instances where your survival mechanism was inappropriately triggered. Make notes here.

_____

_____

_____

_____

_____

_____

What physical symptoms did you experience?

_____

_____

_____

_____

_____

Do you recognize when they are triggered?

_____

_____

_____

_____

MEMORY, RECALL AND EMOTIONS

Some mechanisms of self-control and consciousness relate to emotional memory. Recent neuroscience has identified that emotional memories and memories about emotions are processed, formed and stored differently by the brain. Our brains and behaviour are now coming to rely on computer search engines to give us repeated and consistent answers to our information needs; as a direct result, our elastic brains are storing less information directly because we focus on remembering the location of the information, not the data itself (see References and resources).

It used to be thought that brain design was somewhat inflexible and influenced more by hereditary factors. However, recent research (see References and resources) indicates that the brain is adaptable throughout a person's lifespan, and it is now thought that environmental influences are more significant than genetic ones. Findings suggest that hereditary factors provide between 30 per cent and 60 per cent of our brain's 'hard wiring', while between 40 per cent and 70 per cent is due to environmental factors which are subject to change.

Brain imaging as a tool for research on humans while performing set tasks is gradually rendering out of date the view of the split hemispheres and the dominance of one over the other:

- ▶ left brain hemisphere dominance in speaking, writing and calculations
- ▶ right brain hemisphere dominance in intuitive, creative and spatial matters.

Educators are exploring what can be done to augment left-hemisphere development by boosting the underdeveloped right-hemisphere focus on creativity, complex relationships and spatial patterns. Many more parts of the brain come to the fore in different professions (composer, linguist, artist, mathematician). The longstanding taboo on the use of emotions in business decision-making is also being overturned.

Individuals with brain damage splitting the connection between the hemispheres may continue to be capable of many tasks, but their relationships (and so their lives) fall apart because they cannot make decisions without the emotional centre working with the cognitive centre.

Some of the mystifying things that we do in crises may have been stored and remembered without conscious thought; hence, we reflect in hindsight on what happened as opposed to being able to change our actions in the 'here and now'. If you have ever experienced extreme situations, you may have been surprised that your body carried out some actions without much conscious intervention at the time; you acted before conscious thought about behaviour occurred. The different stages of emotional intelligence development involve moving from hindsight, through mid-sight to foresight so that the emotional roots to behaviour can be predicted.

1 Instinctive reaction comes from the first brain (or reptilian brain) and involves no thinking (cognition) at all. When the hairs on the back of your neck stand up, this is the reptilian brain in action.

2 Hindsight comes from the second brain (or emotional brain) because your thalamus and amygdala had hijacked the stimuli before the neocortex had a chance to form thoughts. Thus, emotion appears to be a precondition for thought and perception, even in cases when we perceive there to be no emotion involved at all.

3 Mid-sight occurs when you catch yourself before an amygdala hijack, bringing yourself back into coherence. To avoid going on full alert each time the senses detect a source of danger, the limbic system evolved a rudimentary

memory recall. It needed to be able to recognize which stimuli were threats and which were not, a pattern-matching process which still underlies our mental functioning today.

4 Foresight comes from the neocortex (the third brain, or cognitive centre) working with the limbic system coherently. Our brains and physiology have to be coherent to be able to predict reactions and choose alternative behaviour. High EQ people act out of foresight, planning for positive emotional outcomes from interactions with one or more people.

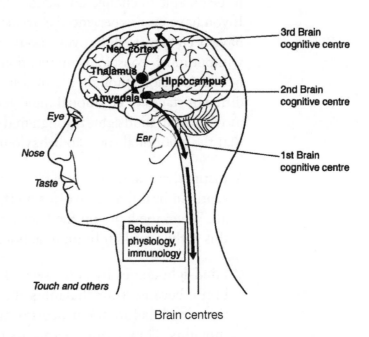

Brain centres

Mid-sight

Identify instances when you recognize that you stopped yourself in the middle of behaving inadvisably. Make notes here.

_____

_____

_____

_____

_____

_____

OUR MEMORY DURING AND AFTER TRAINING OR STUDY

After attending a training event or a period of study, it is important to consolidate the learning using a number of techniques in order to transfer what was learned from the short-term memory to the long-term memory; otherwise, up to 80 per cent of the session content may be lost in the first 24 hours following the event. Hence, it is helpful to prepare for the course, as well as each session, by checking the pre-course material and setting learning expectations. One useful technique is to create a list of questions to be answered. During the sessions, using a mind-mapping technique or a note-taking short-cut can:

▶ aid the brain in creating structure

▶ help to make associations (which is 80 per cent of the way the brain works)

- relate the theory to other constructs, models or practical applications
- identify and enhance the relevance to your role at work
- help to explore applications or anticipated barriers
- relate methods to each other.

Other opportunities come from working with other students and using case studies. These can be evaluated and compared to your own experiences and career progression. The trainer may have related memorable and amusing stories that apply to particular subjects, and you will have generated emotional memories about these. This can help you to transfer the learning to longer-term memory. Such autobiographical memories are often stronger triggers of recall than other types of memory.

My learning experiences

Reflect on a previous training experience and consider what you did immediately after finishing the programme to commit it to memory and make the best use of the training content back at work.

→ How well prepared were you for the event?

_____

_____

_____

_____

→ What was your preferred learning style and how did you absorb the material at the time?

_____

_____

_____

_____

→ How much responsibility did you accept for making the benefits stick in the next few days and weeks?

_____

_____

_____

_____

→ Did your manager, course organizer, mentor or coach assist in the process of finding what makes the short-term memory convert to long-term memory most effectively, and what delivers benefit in your role and overall profession?

_____

_____

_____

_____

→ Were expectations for learning outcomes set prior to going on the course or undertaking some self-study?

_____

_____

As a manager you can ensure that this happens for your staff as a good practice which also ensures value for money.

EXPERIMENTING AND TAKING RISKS

In order to explain unhelpful patterns of behaviour, and to generate better foresight about potentially emotionally charged situations, it is necessary to experiment and try new techniques. These can be coupled with relaxation techniques to further reduce the impact of traumatic events in the past, which can affect the present, limiting the choice of response.

One technique is the APET model, which applies the latest neuroscience knowledge about how emotion precedes reason and perception to achieve more effective development. The **A** in APET stands for activating agent, i.e. any event or stimulus in the environment. Information about that stimulus, taken in through the senses, is processed through the pattern-matching part of the mind (**P**), which gives rises to an emotion (**E**), which *may* inspire certain thoughts (**T**). Some implications are:

▶ Communication with someone in a state of high emotional arousal is impaired. Only when a person is calm can their neocortex employ the subtle 'shades of grey' thinking and reframing abilities that allow the adaptation of patterns and the solving of problems. Therefore, ensuring a person is calm is an essential precondition for effective communication to work.

▶ Some traumatic events are never processed in the neocortex so they cannot be verbalized and rationalized. Any recall of the traumatic event triggers the emotional and physiological responses again without the option for language. Thus, processes which encourage the person to relive or 'talk through' the incident may result in making a traumatic experience more intense.

Each letter of the APET model potentially represents a point of possible change. In some instances, it may be most effective to change the activating agent, i.e. to encourage or to suggest strategies for changing an unsatisfying career or reducing a fear of authority figures.

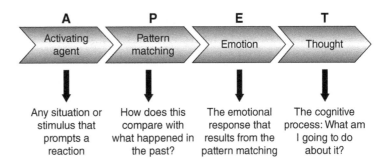

A	P	E	T
Activating agent	Pattern matching	Emotion	Thought
Any situation or stimulus that prompts a reaction	How does this compare with what happened in the past?	The emotional response that results from the pattern matching	The cognitive process: What am I going to do about it?

To give a simple example, a mother may be sitting reading quietly at home when she hears a loud knock on the door. In that instant, the mother experiences inexplicable dread. If she has any conscious thought at all, it is 'Someone's dead!' In the millisecond before her extreme fright, the amygdala had pattern-matched to the time a military policeman knocked at the door to tell her, gently, that her son had been killed on active duty abroad by a roadside bomb during a routine military patrol. If the memory is so emotionally charged that it cannot be healthily processed, it stays trapped in the amygdala as a pre-verbal memory; an event such as loud knocking may trigger post-traumatic stress symptoms such as nightmares, exaggerated startles or panics.

High emotional arousal locks people's focus of attention into a negative trance state where they become confined to viewing the world and their own circumstances from a limiting viewpoint. Learning relaxation techniques to induce a state of deep relaxation reduces the emotional brain's paralysing hold over the neocortex.

It is highly important to work with any unhelpful thoughts or belief patterns (T) which may be holding you back, diminishing your confidence, arousing distress or placing too great a demand on you. When you are relaxed, you can focus attention away from strong emotions; the neocortex can feed a new pattern back to the emotional brain.

Dreaming is a clear example of how the brain is always serving an emotionally driven agenda. Humans experience about five periods of rapid eye movement (REM) sleep a night, during which we dream. Dreams are exact pattern matches to emotionally driven agendas which have not been completed during the day. By providing the pattern match to the emotional arousal, the dream deactivates it, freeing up our thought processes to deal with whatever the new activation agents of the next day will bring.

→ Learning from brain damage examples

Neuropsychological impairments caused by brain injury can be thought of as follows:

▶ intellect, which is the information-handling aspect of behaviour

▶ emotionality, which concerns feelings and motivations

▶ control, which has to do with how behaviour is expressed.

Brain damage rarely affects just one of these systems; rather, the disruptive effects of most brain injuries, regardless of their size or location, usually involve all three systems.

The role of the frontal cortex in personality, specifically in social cognition and executive function, is relatively well-established today, but one of the first pieces of evidence of this role was provided by an industrial accident in the 19th century. In 1848, Phineas Gage, the 25-year-old foreman of a crew of construction workers on a railroad in America, was compacting a borehole with explosive powder using a tamping iron, when a spark ignited the powder, causing the iron to be propelled at high speed straight through Gage's skull. The tamping iron entered under his left cheekbone and exited through the top of his skull, coming to rest 30 yards from the accident. Gage lived for another dozen years but lost his inhibitions; whereas he had been a popular and polite member of the workforce prior to his accident, he became so out of control that he could no longer hold down his position as foreman.

Damage to a specific region of the frontal lobe has been shown to alter people's ability to make moral judgements, leading to a diminished sense of compassion, shame and guilt. In studies where neuro-images of patients' brains showed that they had damage to different parts of the frontal cortex, it was found that what they had in common was damage in the ventromedial prefrontal cortex (VMPC). This is involved in encoding the emotional value of sensory stimuli which generates physiological responses to emotions. The patients all displayed impaired autonomic responses to emotionally charged images, and, in line with previous findings, had a significantly diminished sense of empathy, embarrassment and guilt.

Despite a small sample, the studies provide evidence for the role of emotions, particularly social emotions, in making moral decisions. The differences in the responses of the three groups were greatest when the decisions being made were emotionally charged.

The participants were given situations in which non-moral, personal moral or impersonal moral decisions had to be made, and the results were compared to a control group with no brain damage. Participants were given forced choices where the outcomes were extremely unpleasant for other people (one casualty or five casualties). Other scenarios involved being forced to save their own lives as well as others, which involved hurting or damaging other people, even babies. In this last case, when asked to make personal moral decisions, there was a significant difference between those with damage to the VMPC and those without.

In some fictitious scenarios, the brain-damaged patients were twice as likely to suffocate a noisy baby to save their own or their neighbours' lives from enemy troops. The time taken to make decisions in these high-conflict situations was significantly longer in both groups than the reaction time when making decisions about low-conflict situations.

Thus, the findings confirm the notion that there are at least two neural systems involved in making moral decisions: one in which emotions are involved and one which performs a cost-benefit analysis. It is believed that the emotion-based system for making moral decisions evolved first, perhaps in a situation where small numbers of people lived in groups.

Taking time to reflect on what you have learned in this chapter, summarize your development needs on potential outcomes of your current EQ and plan actions in your personal development plan.

Your PDP

I will start ...

I will do more ...

I will stop ...

I will do less ...

Summary

If you have ever experienced extreme situations, you may have been surprised that your body carried out some actions without much conscious intervention at the time. Some of the mystifying things that we do in crises may have been stored and remembered without conscious thought; hence, we reflect in hindsight on what happened as opposed to being able to change our actions in the 'here and now'.

It is vital to understand the emotional roots of our behaviour if self-directed change is to be successful, and for us to become skilled at self-control. It is also important to have knowledge of recent neuroscience which has identified that emotional memories and memories about emotions are processed differently by the brain. The mechanisms of consciousness and self-control relating to emotional memory are explained further in the following chapters.

3 Developing your self-awareness

Before moving on to the mastery of emotional competence with others, it is essential to achieve personal mastery of the first two categories – self-awareness and self-control. Developing the ability to determine how aware you are of yourself and the repercussions of this awareness is the essential building block of any emotional learning and EQ enhancement.

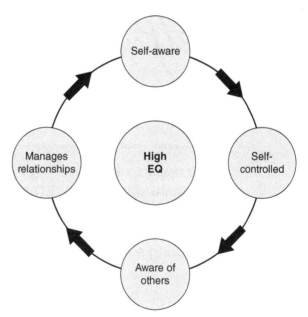

The emotional intelligence cycle

WHAT IT IS

Awareness of feelings: recognizing one's emotions and their effects.

People with this competence:

▶ know which emotions they are feeling, can name and label them

▶ understand the chain from emotion to action (links between their feelings and what they think, do and say)

▶ recognize how their feelings affect their performance, the quality of their experience at work and their relationships

▶ have a guiding awareness of their values or goals and any gap between espoused values and actual behaviour.

self-awareness questionnaire

The results of completing this questionnaire are a very personal view of your EQ because they are self-scored. Each question allows you to estimate the frequency with which you display the competence currently by selecting a score of 1–4 based on the following legend.

Grade	Legend and scoring instructions	Score
Always	There are no exceptions; you would have to think consciously about behaving any other way and changing what you do.	Add 4 points for every tick
Routinely	You would present yourself this way or react this way every week, with few exceptions.	Add 3 points for every tick
Some-times	At your best, this is what you would be seen doing.	Add 2 points for every tick
Rarely	It would be considered unusual for this to be what you say, think or do.	Add 1 point for every tick
Never	There would be no exceptions; you do not present yourself this way to people at any time.	No points

Awareness of feelings

Recognizing one's emotions, the depth of feelings, their effects and the capability to deal with them.

Self-awareness competencies	Never (0)	Rarely (1)	Some-times (2)	Rou-tinely (3)	Always (4)
Do you recognize each of the emotions that you are feeling?					
Can you label them accurately and individually?					
Can you say why you are experiencing those emotions?					
Do you recognize the link from experiencing an emotion to taking action based on it? (e.g. the links between feelings and what you think, do and say)					
Do you recognize when one feeling blocks another emotion?					
Do you recognize how your feelings affect your performance or outcomes?					

Self-awareness competencies	Never (0)	Rarely (1)	Some-times (2)	Rou-tinely (3)	Always (4)
Do you recognize how your feelings affect your work life?					
Do you recognize how your feelings affect the quality of your relationships?					
Do you have a guiding awareness of your values or goals?					
Are you aware of any gaps between your feelings, espoused values and actual behaviour?					

Analyses of the results of your self-assessed score are set out below. Go to the section that matches your score.

Score = 10 or less/predominately answered Never/ Rarely. Achieving this score suggests you may feel that you are living a script written by someone else and that you are not in control of the outcomes of your daily life. You may be puzzled by your relationships with people when they are upset. You may be better at reading other people's feelings than your own – this can arise as a result of some childhood conditioning. There's more on this in the Chapter 11 section on Life scripts.

There are a number of things you can work on. Emotional literacy is the ability to sense single emotions and to label them accurately. To be emotionally literate is to be able to see complex emotions which are blocking raw ones. Connecting with the underlying emotion allows your memory to release information about the root source driving the unproductive behaviour. Your ability to generate foresight rather than having to review your behaviour in hindsight is another. You may transition through mid-sight before you are able to predict a poor performance, catching yourself in the middle of an outburst or bad habit. Use reflection on your day and how you warm yourself up mentally at the start of the day to progress towards your life goals.

With this score the main learning outcome for you is to simplify your life by consistently recognizing the distinction between reality (what actually happened or is happening) and fantasy (interpretation of what happened that, perhaps, generates negative memories or of what may happen in the future that creates negative expectations). You would benefit enormously from working with someone else on developing emotional intelligence.

Score = 11–20/predominately answered Sometimes. Read the self-awareness section and complete the exercises. You have implied that only sometimes can you recognize your emotions, their effects and your capability to deal with them. You may feel that you are unpredictable and that you are not always in control of the outcomes in your daily life. You may be mystified as to what distinguishes one moment of clarity from other times when you are confused, frustrated or even angry and unknowing. These are blanket emotions that disguise your underlying feelings and emotional triggers, which are the clues to your behavioural triggers and bad habits.

Score = 21–30/predominately answered Routinely. You need to explore the reasons why you cannot put 'Always' in all your answers. Identify what throws you out of your routine so that you are not able to identify your feelings. Could it be:

▶ particular people, e.g. parents, a work colleague, a partner?
▶ situations, e.g. lack of trust, being under pressure, in front of authority figures?
▶ events, e.g. New Year reminds you of your ex?

▶ associations, you have an unpleasant association with a colour, smell or object, and you lose focus on the here and now when distracted by it?

Also, did you have a number of 'Never' or 'Rarely' answers? You need to increase your ability to identify triggers that spin you off-course. Look at the analysis above for predominately predominantly 'Never/Rarely' answers and complete the corresponding exercises. Do all of the exercises to get you started on turning your answers into 'Always'. Enrol a colleague in helping you to develop.

Score = 31–40/predominately answered Always. Congratulations, this score reflects a wonderful degree of self-awareness. This characteristic is enormously valuable to you as an individual and if you aspire to be or currently are a leader of others. You have excellent awareness of feelings and this powerful link to your own emotional strengths and frailties means that you are well placed to manage them effectively.

Consider completing some leadership training, as high EQ predisposes you to be very successful and to be able to demonstrate flexible leadership styles for different conditions. After that, reflect on the qualities that you admire in a role model and then explore the characteristics that you feel you have which contribute to your own leadership style. Share with a colleague or reflect on your own, using the results of this to define how you can make your qualities more influential and inspirational.

Consider more emotional self-expression and disclosure to open up team capability and sharing. Trust that the sharing will make you stronger and not more vulnerable with others. This can unlock hidden potential and create a more innovative climate at work.

You should also think about how this strength, if taken to extremes, could become a weakness; for example, pay equal attention to the feelings of others as well as your own by checking out your intuition and displaying empathy.

Check all your self-awareness scores and if others are low then discuss your responses with a colleague or friend. Any self-scored assessment is fallible and worth checking.

Low EQ questionnaire

Complete the table below by identifying how often you display each type of behaviour and ticking the frequency column that applies to you.

Signs of low EQ	Daily	Often	Ad hoc	Rarely	Never
Diversion – you are demonstrating a product to a client but become aware that odd emotions are triggered. For example, you become aware of envy that this person is achieving an unfulfilled ambition of your own.					
Distraction – while you are making a presentation, the audience's body language shows impatience and this is transmitted to you.					

Signs of low EQ	Daily	Often	Ad hoc	Rarely	Never
Internal dialogue – while sitting with a customer, you lose focus and start listening to your inner voice because some aspect of the present is of no interest.					
Interpretation – you turn events in team meetings to mean something about you whereas in reality there is no personal inference at all.					
Withdrawn – withholding knowledge or information is indirect aggressive or passive aggressive behaviour.					
Centre of attention – you have spates of outrageous attention-seeking behaviour with customers.					
Humour - you use it to avoid debating some real issue with the team or client.					
Unfocused – colleagues say something which creates a strong emotion but you avoid addressing it with them.					
Defensiveness – colleagues say something that makes you feel inadequate and you retreat into self-denial, justification or avoidance.					

After completing the low EQ questionnaire, revisit the table using the self-awareness definitions. Even if you do not demonstrate it, consider what might typically be the cost of low EQ.

Spend five minutes reviewing your responses and complete the form below with your gut reaction to your emerging development needs. Write your development needs in the space provided, using the language that will help you in the workplace. Record your thoughts and feelings below and be prepared to discuss the outcomes with your trusted adviser.

→ Give an example of low EQ behaviour.

_____

_____

_____

_____

_____

_____

→ Describe a better outcome.

_____

_____

_____

_____

_____

_____

→ Describe the implications/knock-on effect/cost.

_____

_____

_____

_____

_____

_____

Make a note of the insights your answers have given you.

My development needs

From your self-awareness questionnaire earlier in this chapter, identify and list in the development needs space below a minimum of *three* competencies which are clear strengths.

→ Development needs

1 _____

_____

_____

_____

2 _____

_____

_____

_____

3 _____

_____

_____

_____

4 _____

_____

_____

_____

Identify any 'surprises' that you found when looking at your responses. For each 'surprise', think about which people are in the best position to observe your behaviour associated with each of these competencies. Ask them for feedback using the same rating system, and pay close attention to the ratings of those groups. If you are still surprised by the findings, think about the reasons for their observations.

Raters in best position to observe the competency	Raters' rating of your competency	Possible reasons for 'surprise'
1		
2		
3		
4		

→ Personal outcomes of low EQ

Chapter 2's coverage of brain science and the physiology of performance allowed you to assess the personal outcomes of any low EQ. Here are some examples of low EQ:

▶ you have a poor work/life balance

▶ you are worried, anxious or confused about priorities

▶ you are time-pressured, inefficient and perform poorly

▶ you are tired, fatigued and frustrated

▶ you may have poor health, such as elevated blood pressure

▶ you see premature signs of aging in yourself.

Clearly these are outcomes which are best avoided and may be by raising your EQ.

Summarize your development needs based on the potential outcomes of your low EQ habits; plan actions in your personal development plan that you need to:

▶ start doing

▶ stop doing

▶ do more often

▶ do less often.

Your PDP	
I will start ...	*I will do more ...*
I will stop ...	*I will do less ...*

High EQ

Think of one example of a time when you had a positive emotional response to how well you were handled; for example face-to-face with shop staff. Then recall and think about other examples, such as:

▶ a time when an authority figure had to give you and your colleagues some bad news, which they handled really well, so the experience had a more positive outcome for you

▶ an email or a telephone conversation that left you with a glow, feeling inspired and motivated.

It is important to recall your own experiences. Record them below.

→ Event(s)

_____

_____

_____

_____

_____

_____

_____

_____

Thinking about the event, consider how it compares with the following evidence of high EQ:

▶ I am clear, flexible and collaborative about changing priorities
▶ I reach targets with greater ease and less stress
▶ I am focused, efficient and cool under pressure
▶ I am elated, not tired, and very satisfied at the end of the day
▶ I have a great work/life balance
▶ I am dynamic, and have energy and humour
▶ I look younger than my age.

Ask yourself the following questions and note the insights.

→ Describe an experience of high EQ behaviour in your life.

_____

_____

_____

_____

_____

_____

_____

→ Describe the emotional outcome.

_____

_____

_____

_____

_____

_____

_____

→ Describe the implications/knock-on effect/benefit.

_____

_____

_____

_____

_____

_____

_____

→ **Development planning**

Do I want to develop my emotional intelligence and gain more emotional knowledge, emotional competence and abilities?

_____

_____

_____

_____

What is my personal business case for investment in emotional intelligence discovery and development?

_____

_____

_____

_____

_____

_____

_____

What situations in my life could be alleviated by
managing them in a more emotionally intelligent way?

_____

_____

_____

_____

_____

_____

_____

Based on your competency profile, what would be
the consequences of not taking action in each of the
following areas?

→At home?

_____

_____

_____

_____

_____

_____

→With colleagues?

_____

_____

_____

_____

_____

→In other relationships?

_____

_____

_____

_____

_____

Summary

For many adults, taking time for themselves is not easy, yet this is key to raising your consciousness about your behaviour. You have started this process now and the rest of the book develops this to give you a comprehensive self-test. Once started, most individuals find that making time available is a calming process in their busy life.

Creating the right learning environment may require some negotiation with the people you live with, but having a defined space is likely to be an enormous benefit in forming good study habits.

Learning to trust someone else with this type of emotional learning may be new to you but should quickly prove worthwhile. If the first relationship falters, do not give up; seek another mentor.

4

Developing your self-control

In this chapter we look at self-control – what it is, why it is important and what we can do to improve it.

You will do some exercises to help you to:

▶ *identify your current levels of self-control*
▶ *improve your self-control.*

WHAT IT IS

'I count him braver who overcomes his desires than him who conquers his enemies; for the hardest victory is over self.'

Aristotle

In Chapter 3 you developed your understanding of self-awareness, the fundamental building block of emotional intelligence. The second most important foundation stone of emotional intelligence is self-control.

Self-control is the ability to manage your internal states and impulses so that you achieve desired outcomes in the future. While self-awareness brings these internal states within your cognition, i.e. it makes you aware of them, you have to manage them so that you achieve what you – and others – desire. In Chapter 2, you saw that an amygdala hijack can bring about reactions to triggers that are inappropriate in the circumstances. You can change that by applying self-control.

Self-control is made up of five contributing competencies: self-regulation, authenticity, accountability, flexibility and self-motivation. (Self-motivation is a very important self-control competency and receives separate attention in Chapter 5.)

→ Why developing self-control is important

Having low levels of self-control can seriously damage not only the prospect of you leading a successful life, it can also damage your health. You can become worried, anxious and confused about priorities; you become time pressured, inefficient and perform poorly; you are likely to be tired, fatigued and frustrated and to have a poor work/life balance. And no-one likes people who can't control their negative emotions. (You can probably recall a boss who seemed to be predominately angry and hostile.) You may develop elevated blood pressure and age more quickly, and the risk of developing cancer is also likely to be raised. So developing self-control is very important.

You'll now do an exercise which explains four of the five competencies and assesses your ability to deploy them. The fifth competency (self-motivation) is dealt with in Chapter 5 as it warrants extended treatment.

self-control questionnaire

Read each of the competency descriptions and then tick a single response to each question using the legend as a guide. Add up your score and then select the corresponding score commentary on your present levels of self-control.

Grade	Legend and scoring instructions	Score
Always	There are no exceptions; you would have to think consciously about behaving any other way and changing what you do.	Add 4 points for every tick
Routinely	You would present yourself this way or react this way every week, with few exceptions.	Add 3 points for every tick
Some-times	At your best, this is what you would be seen doing.	Add 2 points for every tick
Rarely	It would be considered unusual for this to be what you say, think or do.	Add 1 point for every tick
Never	There would be no exceptions; you do not present yourself this way to people at any time.	No points

Self-regulation

Managing emotions and holding back unhelpful impulses. To have this competency you would:

▶ stop acting on impulse when it is an unproductive behaviour
▶ remain collected, positive and unflustered even at testing times
▶ manage distressing emotions and reduce anxiety associated with experiencing them
▶ think lucidly, remaining focused under pressure.

	Never (0)	Rarely (1)	Sometimes (2)	Routinely (3)	Always (4)
Are you able to stop acting on impulse?					
Are you able to remain collected, positive and unflustered even at testing times?					
Are you able to identify when your behaviour is unproductive or unhelpful?					
Do you manage distressing emotions well, reducing anxiety associated with these situations?					
Would others say that you are capable of remaining lucid and focused under pressure?					
Sub-total score					

Authenticity

Being true to yourself and others. To have this competency you would:

► build trust through your reliability and congruent behaviour (words and actions are aligned)
► act ethically, being above reproach and questioning of your own motives
► admit flaws and confront unethical actions in others (zero tolerance)
► stand up for your values even when in the minority
► expect yourself to slip back occasionally and have a sense of humour and compassion about it.

	Never (0)	Rarely (1)	Sometimes (2)	Routinely (3)	Always (4)
Are you able to build trust by displaying congruent behaviour, i.e. are your words, body language and actions aligned?					
Would others say you are beyond reproach, act ethically, and are challenging of your own motives?					
Even when in the minority, are you capable of standing up for your values?					
When you slip back into old bad habits, do you have a sense of humour and some compassion about it?					
Sub-total score					

Accountability

Taking responsibility, owning your performance. To have this competency you would:

▶ *take responsibility for your actions and inaction where appropriate*
▶ *clear up miscommunication and keep promises*
▶ *hold yourself accountable to objectives*
▶ *prioritize what is important and urgent every day at work.*

	Never (0)	Rarely (1)	Sometimes (2)	Routinely (3)	Always (4)
Do you take responsibility for your actions and inaction where appropriate?					
Do you clear up assumptions and misconceptions?					
Do you keep promises?					
Do you hold yourself accountable to objectives?					
Would others say that you prioritize what is important or urgent (or both) every day?					
Sub-total score					

Flexibility

Embracing and adapting to change. To have this competency you would:

▶ take account of potential change in your planning
▶ be able to let go, accept shifting priorities and a challenging pace of change
▶ be adaptable in how you perceive events or different people
▶ be open to confronting change issues and exploring the personal implications
▶ take the initiative and be creative in generating and sharing ideas.

	Never (0)	Rarely (1)	Sometimes (2)	Routinely (3)	Always (4)
Do you allow for change in plans and accept the need for some uncertainty?					
Are you capable of letting go of hobby horses and accepting shifting priorities during a challenging period of change?					
Are you adaptable in how you perceive events or different people?					
Are you open to issues that confront you with personal implications?					
Do you explore your personal issues with others?					
Sub-total score					
Total score for all competencies					

Now check the feedback on your overall score below.

Score = 76 to 57. If you have answered most questions as 'Always' or 'Routinely', congratulations! You have a high to exceptional capability to moderate your behaviour.

You would have the ability to reflect on incidents that did not go well and to analyse the chain of emotions which led to unhelpful behaviour. You would recognize when the chain could have been broken and the point at which you could have chosen to behave differently.

If you have achieved this score through a wide variation of responses (0–4), you should also look at the development guidance for the other scores.

Actions to take: With well-developed self-control, you may choose to help others in your circle of influence. Doing so will benefit them and you will also gain from the interactions.

Score = 56 to 38. Well done, you should be pleased with the results. You should as a rule have answered most questions as 'Routinely' or 'Sometimes'. You would benefit from further developing your self-control to bring greater satisfaction to your personal and working lives.

Actions to take: Think back to incidents, perhaps during childhood, that may be leading you in the present day to assign incorrect motives to the behaviour of others. Think about questions that you could ask others in the future to check out what their motive is for their behaviour or their responses to you. In future, try to stop yourself proactively from repeating mistakes. Alternatively, catch yourself in the middle and calm yourself or ask for co-operation in others to avoid a poor outcome. Getting a better result will outweigh any temporary feelings of 'losing face' or 'giving ground'.

Score = 37 to 19. Well done for completing the assessment. You should as a rule have answered most questions as 'Sometimes' or 'Rarely'. The way you act or the responses that you get from others may puzzle you.

You may feel misunderstood a significant amount of the time and not understand what you do that gets you the results that frequently occur. Enlist the help of a friend. Learn to ask for specific feedback from others.

Actions to take: Get into a pattern of preparing for, conducting and reflecting on interactions with people. For example, you may have regular meetings at work, socially or in the community. If you are experiencing regular or ad-hoc difficulties, do some head-clearing before the next event. Get a friend to complete the questionnaire as if they are scoring it about you. Go through the responses and discuss with them what happens to you by reflecting on specific events that you have shared or that have been reported by others.

Score = 18 to 0. Thank you for being so honest. Showing integrity is a great emotional intelligence strength. There is much you can do to improve your self-control and doing so is likely to help you in both your personal and working lives.

Actions to take: You would benefit from completing a course that would help you to increase both your self-awareness and your self-regulation or embarking on a coaching programme. This score does not mean that you necessarily have poor social skills in relating to others, just that you are not particularly aware of how or why you behave the way you do.

Reflection

Reflect on your score and record below two or three specific instances of when you did not achieve the levels of self-control that you would have wished. Recall the environment that prevailed at the time and any negative influences that were acting on you.

→ Describe an instance

_____

_____

_____

_____

→ Describe the environment

_____

_____

_____

_____

→ Negative influences

_____

_____

_____

_____

→ What I would do differently

_____

_____

_____

_____

→ Describe an instance

_____

_____

_____

_____

→ Describe the environment

_____

_____

_____

_____

→ Negative influences

_____

_____

_____

_____

→What I would do differently

_____

_____

_____

_____

→Describe an instance

_____

_____

_____

_____

→Describe the environment

_____

_____

_____

_____

→Negative influences

_____

_____

_____

_____

→What I would do differently

_____

_____

_____

_____

By completing this exercise you may be able to recognize a pattern of behaviour or environmental circumstances that are common to each of the incidents. There may also be a common solution that, when applied, will resolve the issue. Make a note of these in the table below and record them in your journal:

Common behaviour	Common environment	Common solution

Developing your self-control

For each of the self-control competencies in the table below, list your current score and the score that you wish to achieve, and then work out the gap between them, if any. Use the gap to prioritize your list.

Competency	Current score	Desired score	Gap	Priority
Self-regulation				
Authenticity				
Accountability				
Flexibility				

Then in order of priority, briefly describe the actions you will take to reach your goal; make each goal C-SMART, i.e. Challenging, Specific, Measurable, Achievable, Relevant, Time-based

For example:

Priority	Competency	Goal	How I will measure it	Complete by date
3	Authenticity	I will complete a programme of three coaching sessions to enable me to stand by my values even when I feel they are seriously challenged and it would be easier to back down.	I will show my friends and colleagues that I will not compromise on my values by being consistently assertive of my right to stand by my values. They will respect me for my stand.	31 July 2012

Now complete the table below.

Prior-ity	Competency	Goal	How I will measure it	Complete by date
1				
2				
3				
4				

Extract these actions into your personal development plan, which was discussed in Chapter 1, and update your journal to reflect your thinking and reactions to this chapter.

Summary

Self-control is the second of the four fundamental building blocks of emotional intelligence. In this chapter you carried out a self-assessment of the self-control competencies of self-regulation, authenticity, accountability and flexibility. Self-motivation is an important self-control competency which receives separate attention in Chapter 5. You also determined your priorities for developing your self-control as part of an overall personal development plan.

5 Developing your self-motivation

In this chapter we look at self-motivation – what it is, why it is important and what we can do to improve it.

You will complete a negative-belief cycle assessment based on a past experience and an analysis of how you moved on. You'll also do some exercises to help you to:

► *identify your levels of self-motivation*

► *improve your self-motivation.*

WHAT IT IS

'Motivation is the release of power within a person to accomplish some desired result. It is a major key for achievement and success.'

Dr Len Restall

We need motivation on a daily basis to run our lives successfully. Our ability to motivate *ourselves and others* affects our success at work and our satisfaction in life. Motivation is that inner engine that helps us to get up in the mornings and get on with things. It enables us to:

► achieve our goals

► improve our performance

► meet challenges

► cope with change

► be powerful.

The actions that we take are about achieving outcomes that:

▶ keep us safe

▶ give us pleasure

▶ give us reward

▶ avoid an unpleasant experience.

We can be motivated towards or away from an anticipated outcome. When we're motivated towards something, it's because the anticipated outcome will be pleasant or rewarding for us and perhaps also for others. When we're motivated away from something, we are taking action so that we avoid an unpleasant outcome, such as being short of money, being in harm's way or becoming upset.

Our motivation is determined by our attitude to the various external events that impact on our lives. However, our attitude is determined only 10 per cent by outside factors but 90 per cent by our own 'way of being', by the decisions we make based on our upbringing and our experiences. For some of us, our glass is half-full, for others, it's half-empty.

Is your glass half-full or half-empty?

Think now about whether you are a glass half-empty or half-full person. Why is that? Would you like to change anything and why? Make notes below.

→ The type of person I am

_____

→ Why I am that way

_____

_____

→ What I'd like to change and why

_____

_____

_____

_____

_____

That gives you a broad picture of your motivation, but let's look at it in more detail.

My motivation questionnaire

To determine how well motivated you are, complete the questionnaire below. Against each question, score yourself according to the frequency of your behaviour: 'Never' scores 0 and 'Always' scores 4.

Self-motivation

Positively managing your outlook.

	Never (0)	Rarely (1)	Sometimes (2)	Routinely (3)	Always (4)
Are you driven to improve and meet high standards?					
Would people say that you look for the opportunity first before the problem?					
Do you demonstrate commitment in relationships?					
Do you explore barriers and boundaries in relationships?					
Do you show persistence in overcoming setbacks?					
Do you show persistence in pursuing positive outcomes?					
Do you actively seek to overcome things which cause you dissatisfaction?					
Do you reflect on what motivates you to achieve things?					
Do you manage relationships based on how they affect your self-motivation?					
Do you intervene if others try to drag you down?					
Total score					

Now check the feedback on your score.

Score = 10 or less. Thank you for your honesty. The good news is that you can radically improve your self-motivation. Just how you go about doing that depends on the source of your negative influences as they are almost certainly the cause of your apparent lack of self-motivation. Carry on reading this chapter and complete all of the exercises.

Score = 11–20. Congratulations, you already have the foundations of high self-motivation. You just need to develop this important skill so that you really can have an impact on your own life and those of your colleagues. The real power of self-motivation lies in your ability to bounce back and maintain a positive image of yourself. Carry on reading this chapter and complete all of the exercises.

Score = 21–30. Congratulations, you already have well-developed self-motivation. However, you might wish to develop it further in the realization that the real power of self-motivation lies in your ability to bounce back and maintain a positive image of yourself. In so doing, you'll reduce stress and live a happier, more balanced life. Carry on reading this chapter and complete all of the exercises.

Score = 31–40. Well done, you have excellent self-motivation which will stand you in good stead in your work and personal relationships. Through the power of self motivation, you:

▶ will be driven to improve or meet high standards
▶ demonstrate commitment in all your relationships
▶ will look for the opportunity first, not the problem
▶ show persistence in pursuing goals and intentionality in overcoming barriers or setbacks.

You may wish to buddy up with others to help them towards achieving the same levels of motivation as you have. That would be great for them – and for you too.

→ ## It's complex

Motivation is a complex subject. It has been, and continues to be, the subject of considerable research. It is complex for many reasons, not least of which is that different people are motivated by different things and in different ways. Some motivators are common to most of us: the need for safety; the need for food and water; the need for shelter; the need for companionship and love; the need for recognition. As well as these needs, there are also 'wants', which are not necessary for our survival yet we pursue them because we choose to, for whatever reason.

MASLOW'S HIERARCHY OF NEEDS

There are many models of motivation but we'll concentrate here on a commonly used one, Maslow's hierarchy of needs.

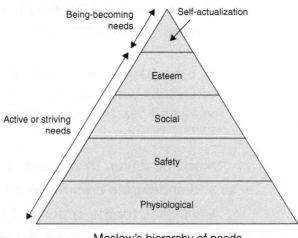

Maslow's hierarchy of needs
(satisfied needs no longer motivate behaviour)

Maslow listed motivating factors based on needs as:

▶ physiological – hunger, thirst, warmth, etc.
▶ safety – home, job, etc.
▶ social – a need to belong, have friends, be accepted, be liked, etc.
▶ esteem – your worth or importance, recognition, a feeling of accomplishment, a job well done, a large house, a large car, etc.
▶ self-actualization – more of a person, more mature, more concerned for others, paying back into society, etc.

Maslow postulated that when our physiological needs are satisfied, we move on up the hierarchy to the next level. Although these needs are shown in the diagram above as a hierarchy, we know that they do not exist in isolation of one another, but in varying proportions according to where we think we are currently within the triangle, as shown in the diagram below.

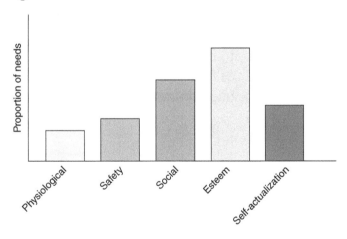

Maslow's hierarchy in proportion

You need to be aware that, once you have moved up through the hierarchy of needs, you will not necessarily stay where you are. Internal and external factors can force you back down again. For example, in a recession and its aftermath, many people will lose their jobs. So the safety factor becomes more important and perhaps some of the physiological factors as well. The same person would therefore automatically adjust their basic needs to take account of their changed position.

My hierarchy of needs

Now think about where you are in the hierarchy of needs; think about where you want to be; and start to think about what you will have to do to get there. Be realistic and honest – try to get an accurate picture of your current situation; and remember that when a need is satisfied, it becomes relatively small in proportion to other needs.

In the following table, mark with an X where you are on the scale for each need; mark with an O where you want to be. The table includes a SAMPLE column with scores of 5 for current and 8 for future. You may find it helpful to use different colours for the X and O.

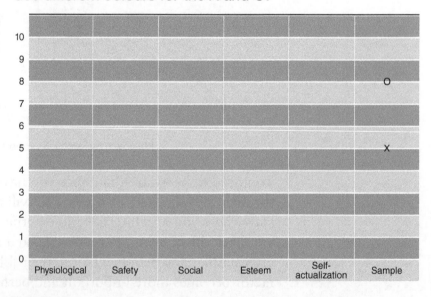

→ Work out the gap between your X and O for each factor (the score) and write it below:

Physiological _____

Safety _____

Social _____

Esteem _____

Self-actualization _____

→ Rank your scores for each factor, with the highest score first:

1st _____

2nd _____

3rd _____

4th _____

5th _____

Now in a couple of sentences, write down what you have learned about yourself from these exercises and what you will do as a result.

→ What I have learned from the Maslow exercise

_____

_____

_____

_____

→ What I plan to do

_____

_____

_____

_____

_____

_____

_____

→ # The mind/body link

The mind/body link is a powerful driver of behaviour.
Your behaviours are driven by your thoughts, which are
influenced by your perceptions, your emotions and your
beliefs.

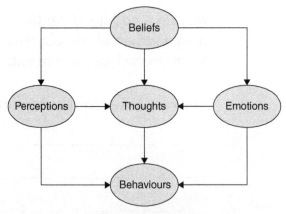

The mind/body link

If your thinking on a topic is influenced by predominately
negative perceptions, emotions or beliefs, then your
behaviour is likely to be 'negative' too, reinforcing a

negative-belief cycle. For motivation to work, you need a positive mental attitude, not a negative mental attitude.

→ The negative-belief cycle

All of us have experienced negative memories at some point in our lives. When they arise, we have a choice about whether we deal with them in a positive or a negative way. We can follow the cycle from the memory of, for instance, an occasion when we messed up, expecting that we will do the same again in the belief that we can't do other than whatever it was that went wrong. That negative belief then impacts on our performance in a negative way and we think that we'll be punished in some way.

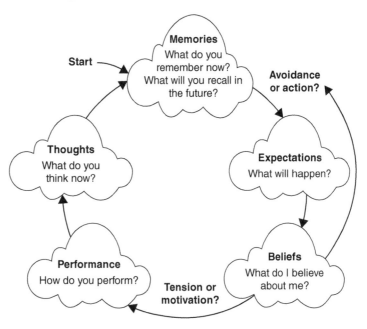

Alternatively, we can recall the memory and the associated expectations and beliefs and decide to take action to improve our performance and result in positive thinking about the situation. So we can move from a negative to a positive attitude.

From negative to positive

Think now of a negative memory of an occurrence you would rather not experience again. In the table below, record how you will move from the negative aspects that you experienced in the negative-belief cycle to a positive-belief cycle:

Negative memory	What will I recall in the future to make it positive?
What action did I take, if any?	What action will I now take?
What did I expect to happen?	What do I now expect to happen?
What did I believe about me?	What do I now believe about me?
How did this motivate me?	How will this now motivate me?

How did I perform?	*How will I now perform?*
What did I think then?	*What do I think now?*
What enduring change will I see?	

→ Ten top motivational tips

So how do we get ourselves motivated and stay that way?

1 Develop and maintain a positive mental attitude. There really is nothing more powerful for self-motivation than a positive attitude to all that we undertake and encounter. When negativity knocks on the door, open the door and immediately reframe it into something positive. Although you can't control every circumstance in your life, you can choose your attitude towards them. Use the exercises in this chapter to shift from a negative to a positive mental attitude.

2 Surround yourself with motivational things: things that make you smile, make you laugh, make you recall great events in your life. They might be pieces of music or artwork, people or objects with happy associations – anything that gives you a lift.

3 Be open-minded. A closed mind is a shut-down life. Seek out new experiences, new relationships, new learning. Warmly embrace new opportunities that will expand your way of being.

4 Focus on your way of being, not your way of doing. People relate to you not because of *how* you do things but because of *who* you are, through the principles by which you lead your life.

5 Be less reactive and more active. Set yourself short-term (say, three-month), medium-term (one-year) and long-term (3–5 year) goals. Make them relevant and C-SMART.

  ▷ Challenging. Your goals need to stretch you, but not too far (see 'Achievable'): too easy and they will not motivate you to better things; too difficult and you risk becoming demotivated.

  ▷ Specific. Your goals need to be specific, not vague or rambling. Use powerful 'action' words and address who, what, when, where and how. For example, 'I will lose 3 kg in weight within six weeks by exercising for one hour every day either at home or in a gym, and through better controlling my diet by eating less carbohydrate'. And each goal needs to reinforce the others so that your short-term goals feed into your medium- and long-term agenda.

  ▷ Measurable. Know where you started from and where you want to get to. Measure your progress along the way.

  ▷ Achievable. To remain motivated, your goals must be achievable, i.e. although they should stretch you, they represent something that you can achieve in terms of your interest, energy, ability, financial capacity and timescale.

  ▷ Relevant. Relevance is essential. Your goal must be relevant to what you want to achieve. If you have a series of goals, each must contribute to your overall aim. If goals are not relevant, they are a distraction and a waste of time and energy. It's also important that you revisit them regularly to ensure that they remain relevant.

▷ Time-based. Every goal needs to have a timescale, otherwise you could drift along in the right direction but never get there.

6 Be accountable for your own action or inaction; we all need to be responsible for our own outcomes. It's easy to blame others or external events for upsetting our chosen path, but life is guaranteed to get in the way from time to time. Acknowledge that and adjust as necessary.

7 Don't be afraid to change what you do. If you always do what you've always done, then expect to always get what you always got. It's good to 'think outside the box', take a fresh look and adopt a fresh approach.

8 **When you make progress, reward yourself. The rewards** don't have to be great, but they must be meaningful and appealing. Vary them because variety is the spice of life.

9 Build your confidence. Make a list of all of your strengths and past successes, and all the things in your life that are good; don't forget loves, relationships, hobbies, interests. Reflect on why they are/were successful or why they make you feel good. When you're setting your goals, have a look at your list and use it to inspire your thinking.

10 Finally, and perhaps most importantly, when your motivation is low, just get on and do something about it. You have a dream to believe in, now live that dream.

Summary

In this chapter, you examined what self-motivation is and what drives it. You saw how it enables you to:

▶ achieve your goals

▶ improve your performance

▶ meet challenges

▶ cope with change

▶ be powerful

You learned that the actions you take are about achieving outcomes that:

▶ keep you safe

▶ give you pleasure

▶ give you reward

▶ avoid an unpleasant experience

You looked at Maslow's hierarchy of needs and did an exercise to establish where you are within the hierarchy and what you would change. You learned about the importance of the mind/body link and how it impacts on the negative-belief cycle.

Exercises helped you to embed these concepts into your thinking and led you towards taking action to improve your self-motivation. Finally, ten self-motivation tips reinforced your way forward.

6

Developing your awareness of others

Another foundation block of emotional intelligence is awareness of others. On a person-to-person level, being aware of others includes empathy, which is distinct from showing sympathy to another person. In an organizational context, being aware of others includes having a service orientation, which is critical for many public and private sector operations.

WHAT IT IS

People who are aware of others have good social awareness, recognizing the intensity and nature of emotions in other people by noticing their emotional cues. People with this ability recognize the facial expressions, eye movement, posture, gestures, tone of voice and other physical manifestations, such as stress symptoms (sweating, dry mouth, uneven breathing), that others have. Using these observations empathically, they can adjust their behaviour and body language accordingly to achieve rapport, aiding communication quality. By having well-practised active listening skills, they appreciate both what is said and why it is being said.

Discovering the consequences of low awareness of others and how it manifests itself is a useful addition to your personal development plan. The benefit and impact that higher levels of awareness have on different areas of your life is worth identifying.

As you can see from the charts in the diagram below, developing capability in empathy and service orientation builds on the individual capabilities of self-awareness and self-control. They complement becoming more politically intelligent and influential in an organization, topics covered in later chapters.

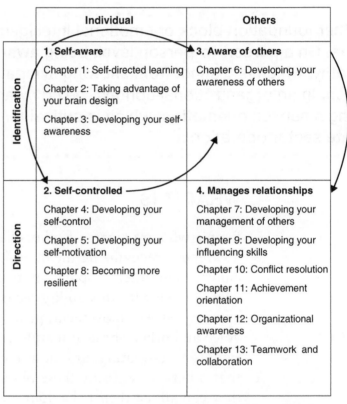

	Individual	Others
Identification	**1. Self-aware** Chapter 1: Self-directed learning Chapter 2: Taking advantage of your brain design Chapter 3: Developing your self-awareness	**3. Aware of others** Chapter 6: Developing your awareness of others
Direction	**2. Self-controlled** Chapter 4: Developing your self-control Chapter 5: Developing your self-motivation Chapter 8: Becoming more resilient	**4. Manages relationships** Chapter 7: Developing your management of others Chapter 9: Developing your influencing skills Chapter 10: Conflict resolution Chapter 11: Achievement orientation Chapter 12: Organizational awareness Chapter 13: Teamwork and collaboration

The scope of emotional intelligence in this workbook

For each 'Aware of others' competency in the following diagram, consider the link with each of the competencies in the other quadrants and add actions to your personal development plan.

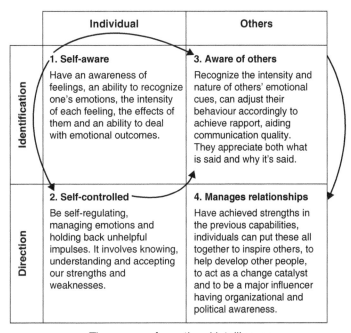

	Individual	Others
Identification	**1. Self-aware** Have an awareness of feelings, an ability to recognize one's emotions, the intensity of each feeling, the effects of them and an ability to deal with emotional outcomes.	**3. Aware of others** Recognize the intensity and nature of others' emotional cues, can adjust their behaviour accordingly to achieve rapport, aiding communication quality. They appreciate both what is said and why it's said.
Direction	**2. Self-controlled** Be self-regulating, managing emotions and holding back unhelpful impulses. It involves knowing, understanding and accepting our strengths and weaknesses.	**4. Manages relationships** Have achieved strengths in the previous capabilities, individuals can put these all together to inspire others, to help develop other people, to act as a change catalyst and to be a major influencer having organizational and political awareness.

The scope of emotional intelligence

→ Empathy

Empathic individuals understand other people and take an active interest in issues facing them. Empathy is about being aware of other people's feelings and being able to guess what others are thinking but not saying. By having active listening skills, empathic people accurately hear and understand the unstated or partially expressed thoughts, feelings and concerns of others. The depth of understanding of others may include cross-cultural sensitivities (see References and resources), useful when working in a diverse or multi-national organization.

Everyone needs greater empathy in society; society suffers for the lack of it. Individuals low in empathy may express frustration that they are 'unable to fathom other people', such as team members and family members. If this is the case, the likely consequences are that they make decisions or take actions without seeking feedback on the opinions and preferences of those around them. As leaders, they may appear autocratic and dismissive or indifferent and uncaring.

Being on your own agenda	Being on your staff's agenda
Opinion	Listening
Sympathizing	Being there
Advice	Empathizing
Coping strategies	Helping strategies

The table above illustrates noticeable differences in attitude between an individual focused on their own agenda rather than of their staff. It would be difficult for a leader with little empathy to succeed by setting targets and achieving goals with and through a team of people. Having a high staff turnover in a team may be an indicator of this development need.

Finding a good role model for empathy is an excellent way to observe the behaviour (to know what 'good' looks like) and to discuss all aspects of acquiring it. Part of this process is identifying the benefit to you of looking at your current life and how it may change into a better quality life/work balance for yourself and others around you.

Signs of a lack of empathy involve compartmentalizing the people in your life and making assumptions about their feelings, the reasons for their actions, and what they want or say. Frequent misunderstandings may occur where there is little empathy, with individuals expressing concern that they are surrounded by 'difficult people'.

As a result, conflict may arise and there is the likelihood of little capability to resolve the grievances on either side, with both parties lacking the ability to express their needs and suggest considerate ways forward. There may be a lack of awareness of the contribution made by others or reluctance to acknowledge their involvement.

→ Service orientation

People with this capability are evidently working on the agenda of others more than their own; typically, they are clear about the business goal in serving others. Therefore, the person demonstrates a desire to help or serve others in order to meet a customer's needs. This capability includes the skill to elicit requirements as well as eagerly meet them, and being proactive in adding value to help each customer. They take personal responsibility for achieving the customer's desired outcome and may make excellent account managers. This effort can result in sustainable, profitable relationships with customers.

Where an organization's culture rewards service orientation, individuals with this strength will thrive. Reward mechanisms that recognize their contribution will reinforce the service orientation capability. Taking extra effort to ensure customer satisfaction can lead to advocacy and a subsequent low cost of acquisition of new customers through recommendation and referral. This capability is often seen as essential to sales and marketing roles but it also underpins the attitudes and behaviours of good people managers.

Issues arise when people have a role that requires high levels of awareness of others, yet they lack the competence. Typically, these will manifest themselves as complaints from staff, peers, suppliers and customers regarding a mismatch of promises, expectation and delivery. Equally, the individual may complain about their customers. Individuals may set targets that ignore client needs and deliver mundane or 'off the shelf' solutions.

People without good social awareness will appear uncaring about how client work is done. They may focus on their own agenda and remain unaware of what a customer needs.

Service orientation is a capability which benefits from close monitoring by supervisors and managers as it will impact on the bottom line adversely when the capability is weak. A supportive environment where mutually set expectations and targets are reviewed regularly is likely to be more conducive to achieving positive outcomes. This development area would benefit from exploration with a trusted adviser, along with achievement orientation and organizational awareness, particularly where all three competencies are important to your role.

Here are a number of practical exercises to help you demonstrate being aware of others and to develop excellent social awareness capabilities.

→ Active listening

Words are spoken to you at a rate of 90–200 words a minute. Thought is faster than speech by a magnitude of 3–7 times. Emotions are processed 80,000 times faster than thoughts, so we respond emotionally before we respond rationally to others' speech. The plodding speaker is using a fraction of our attention; therefore, hungry for activity, our mind wanders.

When two people are in conflict, the conversation has to move one step at a time, ensuring that both people have a clear and common understanding of what is happening. This is because when human beings are under stress, they hear what they want to hear and not necessarily what is being said.

One of the most powerful things we can do for another human being is to focus our attention on them. When an individual feels acknowledged in this way by a calm individual who sits without distraction, it engenders beneficial physiology in both the listener and the speaker. Active listening demonstrates self-awareness, self-control, being aware of others and having respect for what another individual is saying.

Please try experiencing active listening for yourself. The aim is to deepen communication between you and others through you listening to the best of your ability. *Do not* pick a top stressor, which may divert you from learning.

▶ A listener keeping a positive frame of mind listens attentively and gives short, accurate summaries of what has been heard.
▶ A speaker confirms (or not) that the listener has understood. When understood, the speaker continues.
▶ The listener concentrates on quietening their inner voice, warmly appreciating the speaker, increasing intuition and empathy. Here, the listener is seeking to ensure that the speaker feels heard and understood.

How often do we listen twice as much as we talk?

Active listening role play

Try the following role play.

Person A speaks to Person B, describing a change, issue or challenge that might be causing them moderate to high stress. Take a minute to bring the issue to mind and strongly imagine it before speaking. Allow yourself to experience the emotions it engenders but not the behaviour. In other words, you can feel anger but not behave aggressively as an angry person might. Recognize the stress engendered, the feelings of anxiety.

Person B listens to what is being said, then verbally summarizes it. Allow the speaker a minute to think about the issue. Arrange your body into an open posture and clear your mind of what is going on for you. Concentrate on the other person without staring at them.

Person A confirms that person B has understood their statement, or clarifies what has been misunderstood or overlooked.

When Person A is understood, he or she continues.

If Person B has missed something, he or she summarizes again what Person A has said.

Person A confirms that Person B has understood.

As you go through this exercise, it is critical that you follow all of the steps. You may feel at times that this moves very slowly, or that the person understands so you can skip a step or two. That is a mistake. In a difficult situation, no matter how slow and redundant you feel the process is, stick to it until you have common understanding (even if, once they understand, the other person doesn't agree).

Break off active listening and pick up development ideas in the following ways.

▶ Summarize, physically shifting position, and ask questions.

- ▶ Ask if it is appropriate to move forward.
- ▶ The listener was supposed to invoke positive emotions of appreciation and warmth in the speaker without saying anything and was to disregard any negative emotions which crept into his or her mind. Was this achieved?
- ▶ The listener was supposed to practise their listening on the basis of mutual respect (quieting their ego and their urge or need to speak), utilizing their self-awareness (being aware of their feelings) and self-control (quietening the inner voice) to improve the quality of listening. Was this achieved?
- ▶ Swap roles and, if possible, use an observer to get feedback on the performance of both Person A and Person B roles.

This technique can be applied to groups or individuals and can be used to resolve conflict as well as to demonstrate authenticity and accountability (self-control competencies). Using positive emotions increases intuition and empathy, enabling you to make more associations from what you hear and to share these with the speaker (received as reading between the lines intuitively or being perceptive). Make notes on the degree to which you listened effectively (as Person B) and how successfully you experienced being heard (as Person A).

RAPPORT

Creating rapport with another person or a group involves an alignment of body language and other physical manifestations of our mental state, such as the intensity of emotion in our voice, its pitch, volume and musicality. Therefore, by mimicking someone else's physiology we can hasten rapport.

Mirroring occurs when one person's physiology is the mirror of the person with whom he or she has rapport. For example, one person may have their left leg crossed over the right and be leaning to the right. The other will have his or her right leg crossed over the left and is leaning to the left.

Matching is more likely to occur when two people in rapport are sitting next to each other rather than opposite each other. In this case, both would have, for example, their left leg crossed over the right and the chin resting on the right hand.

However, what would you do if you wanted to achieve rapport with someone who used very expansive body language? Were you to copy them exactly, you could well cause offence, especially in multicultural situations. Conversely, if you do not copy them at all, then achieving a state of rapport could take much longer. The solution is to copy their movements with less exaggerated ones of your own, perhaps copying an arm movement with your hand or even just a finger. This is called 'cross-over mirroring' or 'cross-matching'.

How do you know when rapport is established? Having matched or mirrored the person you wish to gain rapport with, you can test how you are doing by 'leading' and 'pacing'. What this means is that instead of continuing to copy them, you make a different movement of your own and see if they copy you. If they do, then you have established rapport and you now have the optimum conditions for influencing them and gaining their co-operation.

If they do not follow you, then continue to pace their body language for a while and then test again to see if you are being copied by them yet.

These are the more obvious signs of rapport, yet there are many other ways of achieving rapport with someone. By knowing what these ways are and how to activate them, you can speed up the process of achieving rapport, which your conscious mind has commenced, enabling a friendly, co-operative atmosphere to develop in the minimum of time.

▶ Matching someone's breathing rate is a very effective way of gaining rapport quickly, such as in calming a baby. When you laugh, it involves a very particular way of breathing, almost panting, and when you see two people laughing together, you know that they are in rapport.

▶ Eye contact is essential in achieving effective communications with another person. It also demonstrates that you are listening. In particular, matching their blink rate is an extremely powerful way of gaining rapport.

Try this out next time you find yourself in a busy pub or bar. If you have been waiting for some time to get served, try this simple exercise. Hold a banknote between the second and third finger of your raised hand. Watch the bartender's rate of blinking and match it, twitching the note up and down about an inch in time with his or her blink rate. You are likely to be the next person he or she serves, unless, of course, everyone else is using the same technique!

Empathy questionnaire

The following self-assessment will give you an opportunity to reflect on your current degree of empathy, i.e. how aware you are of the emotions of others. There are a number of things that occur to people with low empathy in terms of how they are perceived by others. This can lead to you feeling misunderstood or out of tune with others, which is uncomfortable. Use the table below to identify your strengths and development needs, and then think of some strategies for increasing empathy.

Grade	Legend and scoring instructions	Score
Always	There are no exceptions; you would have to think consciously about behaving any other way and changing what you do.	Add 4 points for every tick
Routinely	You would present yourself this way or react this way every week, with few exceptions.	Add 3 points for every tick
Sometimes	At your best, this is what you would be seen doing.	Add 2 points for every tick
Rarely	It would be considered unusual for this to be what you say, think or do.	Add 1 point for every tick
Never	There would be no exceptions; you do not present yourself this way to people at any time.	No points

Awareness of others
Recognizing the emotional cues and the depth of emotion that others are feeling and thinking but not saying.

	Never (0)	Rarely (1)	Some-times (2)	Routinely (3)	Always (4)
Do you recognize each of the emotions that others are feeling?					
Can you identify the emotions of others and label them accurately?					
Can you identify why others are experiencing those emotions?					

Awareness of others

Recognizing the emotional cues and the depth of emotion that others are feeling and thinking but not saying.

	Never (0)	Rarely (1)	Some-times (2)	Routinely (3)	Always (4)
Do you adjust your behaviour in response to others' feelings?					
Do you recognize distinct facial expressions in others?					
Do you recognize when someone is emotionally conflicted with a primary emotion blocking an underlying feeling, and showing stress reactions?					
Do you have well-honed active listening skills?					
Can you achieve rapport with others?					
Can you deal with the exaggerated body language of others and achieve rapport?					
Are you able to lead and pace those people that you have achieved rapport with?					

We have encouraged you to develop a personal development plan. Consider the following and then add to your personal development plan the things that you need to start doing to demonstrate greater empathy.

► The things you do that block empathy or break rapport with others.
► The things you need to do more or less often.
► Even if you do not demonstrate it, what is the cost of low empathy typically?

Empathy

Record your thoughts and feelings below and be prepared to discuss the outcomes with your trusted adviser.

→ Give an example of low empathy.

_____

_____

_____

_____

_____

_____

_____

→ Describe a better outcome.

_____

_____

_____

_____

_____

_____

_____

→ Describe the implications/knock-on effect/cost.

_____

_____

_____

_____

_____

_____

_____

Make notes of the insights in the space below.

→ Development needs

1 _____

_____

_____

_____

_____

_____

_____

_____

2 _____

_____

3 _____

_____

_____

_____

_____

_____

_____

_____

4 _____

_____

_____

_____

5 _____

_____

_____

_____

_____

_____

_____

_____

_____

Keep a log of situations in which you feel you demonstrated empathy at the levels that you have set as targets; log times when you did not show it and describe any environmental or relationship factors which may have contributed to this. Set your own list and get feedback on the things that you need to start doing, stop doing, do more or do less often.

Your PDP	
I will start ...	*I will do more ...*
I will stop ...	*I will do less ...*

In reviewing your actual performance, pay particular attention to critical incidents that provided opportunities for you to identify underlying concerns that are not explicitly expressed by others. Tune into the emotions that others are expressing.

Create good habits to enable you to take note of your empathy capability, such as reviewing at the end of the day whether you were engaged appropriately.

▶ Grade your performance: did you listen to someone who approached you to express his or her feelings or did you appear too busy to talk to them and brush the person off?

▶ Were you asking people open-ended questions: what, when, where, why, how?

▶ Did you practise using open-ended questioning to enable you to confirm that you understood the other person's point of view fully, in terms of feelings, context and content?

- ▶ What were your rapport skills like with others? Do your skills go up and down depending on what you feel about the other person or what you believe they think of you?
- ▶ What did you learn about other people: their motivation, cultural differences, preferences, predisposition, background, different values and beliefs and did you adjust your response accordingly?

If you do not frequently show empathy, identify any personal obstacles so that you may set goals for improving your performance; for example, if you find that you score highly on achievement orientation, this may need balancing with your need to be more empathic. A background in task-oriented professions such as engineering or IT may mean that taking time to listen to others' problems may seem a lower priority.

Please discuss issues with a trusted adviser or mentor. You should organize an appraisal which takes into account progress and barriers with this important competence. When you work on your own, you may work systematically through a number of resources (see References and resources) to improve your skills.

Service orientation

Take an action to suggest changes to a company procedure that a customer has complained about.

- ▶ Keep a log of situations in which you observed evidence of effective service orientation demonstrated by others. What were the patterns of behaviour you observed? Ask others what they were thinking about when they took those actions.

▶ Practising the thoughts and behaviours of effective service orientation enables you to learn and master the competency. A good way to organize that practice is to set a specific goal and action plan for enhancing the service relationship you have with your customers.

▶ Set a measurable goal to improve the level of service you have provided to your customers. Include a needs analysis, an analysis of your service compared to competitors, and an analysis of the concerns of your customers.

▶ Construct a plan of action to deliver a new and better service to your customers. Reality-test the plan and the outcome you want with your manager or a colleague.

▶ Start a reading file of articles about your customers and their needs.

Which aspect of service orientation would be most valuable in helping you to perform more effectively? How would strengths in other competencies help? Identify three or four links between empathy and this competence, describing why it would help. Which competencies covered in other chapters are at strength and which would be most valuable in helping you to perform this behaviour more effectively, e.g. achievement orientation and organizational awareness?

Underpinning competency	How this would help

Summary

The chapter begins the process of developing greater emotional intelligence with others, building on awareness and self-control. Ask yourself the following questions after using the exercises in this chapter.

▶ When you listen to other people, are you waiting for your chance to speak?

▶ In the company of others, do you appear in harmony with them or is there something unspoken which is not going right?

▶ Are you aware of what others are feeling and thinking but not saying?

▶ Do you act on the agenda of the person being served or are you solely serving your own goals?

Update your personal development plan according to your responses.

7 Developing your management of others

This chapter focuses on the relationship management skills shown in the diagram below, i.e. equipping you to develop others, to be an inspirational leader, to catalyse change and gain momentum; and to be a great team member as well as engendering teamwork and collaboration in others.

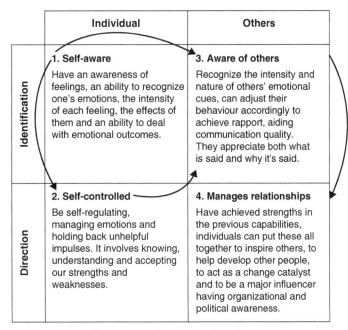

	Individual	Others
Identification	**1. Self-aware** Have an awareness of feelings, an ability to recognize one's emotions, the intensity of each feeling, the effects of them and an ability to deal with emotional outcomes.	**3. Aware of others** Recognize the intensity and nature of others' emotional cues, can adjust their behaviour accordingly to achieve rapport, aiding communication quality. They appreciate both what is said and why it's said.
Direction	**2. Self-controlled** Be self-regulating, managing emotions and holding back unhelpful impulses. It involves knowing, understanding and accepting our strengths and weaknesses.	**4. Manages relationships** Have achieved strengths in the previous capabilities, individuals can put these all together to inspire others, to help develop other people, to act as a change catalyst and to be a major influencer having organizational and political awareness.

The scope of emotional intelligence

WHAT IT IS

A number of us are naturally good managers of other people; many are not. It is not unusual to become a people manager when your true focus is on career progression, pay and remuneration. You may feel sometimes that you do not have the skills needed to meet these new challenges. Many of us have experienced this at one time or another; you feel as if you will be 'found out' after being promoted (known as the imposter syndrome). You may be surprised at the number of famous people, some great achievers, who have admitted to feeling this way.

If you are new to management, then first impressions can be important and so can the physical environment in which you interact with people. There are practical aspects to equipping you to develop others, to be inspirational, catalyse change, gain momentum, and engender teamwork and collaboration. For example, do you have suitable spaces affording privacy where you can develop other people? Does the organization provide unified communications so that you have bottom to top communications as well as top to bottom messages? Have you anywhere suitable to hold team events without disturbing others in order to transfer excellence around the team.

It is important for you to discover the benefits of having high EQ in these capabilities and the consequences of these not being at strength, so that you are positively motivated to try to improve. How do your capabilities in relationship management manifest themselves to others? Do you have mechanisms for establishing the impact that you have on others? This can be simply making the time to talk openly together.

Survey evidence suggests that having an effective process of two-way communication is a key driver of employee engagement. A 2006 study by Kingston Business School (Truss) found, for example, that 'allowing people the opportunity to feed their views and opinions upwards is the single most important driver of engagement' and that 'keeping employees informed about what is going on in the organization is critical'. A supporting study established that line managers are key to employees' engagement, which reinforces the need to meet their priorities. These are:

▶ to have change managed very well

▶ to feel more empowered

▶ to understand their contribution to the strategy

▶ to be motivated and inspired to do their best work

▶ to be treated fairly

▶ to feel proud to tell others where they work.

So, to create an environment for others to succeed, what does this mean about you? Who or what will you have to do or be in order to achieve the right climate at work? The answers to these questions are all ones which should result in an entry in your personal development plan as they occur to you. Record them on a readily available source: mobile phone, iPad, laptop or paper.

Another factor considered by employees to be essential is the authenticity of leaders. Authentic leadership was first written about following research by Rob Goffee and Gareth Jones at the London Business School. They wrote a book called *Why Should Anyone Be Led by You* about what it takes to be an authentic leader. The messages in the book resoundingly emphasize the emotional intelligence of a leader. You need to know yourself and to be yourself. You need to have the awareness to understand that what works for one person will not necessarily work for another. You also need to accept and work with modern expectations that leaders should be non-hierarchical and contextual, i.e. adaptable and changing their styles of leadership depending on the circumstances.

→ Developing others

Investing in other people's capabilities is at best an altruistic act. In the world of business or in public service, developing people can be about achieving results and controlling behaviour at work (sticking to the company competency profile, for instance). Are you the sort of person who likes to develop the capabilities of other people? This ability includes making a long-term commitment to facilitating the development of others, such as by acquiring and using coaching and mentoring skills. This is not to be confused with training people.

Tell people in what capacities you expect them to excel and have specific evidence of what they did and how they did it. Practise giving specific, behavioural feedback, making sure you are commenting on their successes. Offer support to help them develop their capability further where there is room for improvement. It is useful to be able to demonstrate to other employees what 'good' looks like when congratulating a team member.

Hold regular meetings with your staff to discuss their progress and how you can help with their development, while ensuring that each employee takes ownership of his or her development plan. Give employees time on their own to formulate plans of work by providing them with the overall objective and letting them identify how to carry it out. Distinguish between short-, medium- and long-term development objectives; for each timescale in turn, focus on threading three-year goals back to the actions needed in the present. Each big goal may need interim objectives; only intervene if the employee is not accountable for progress.

Where it is feasible within their role, expand their horizons by, for instance, letting them attend conferences on your behalf, submit papers or become a speaker. They may need a lot of encouragement but it will fast-track their progress. Generate a more interesting mix of work as often as possible, such as project work as well as their usual tasks. Introduce them to others as often as possible and encourage them to network. Deputize someone to undertake your role during absences from the office as required. Stretch them by giving them (limited) decision-making authority so that the deputizing role represents a real delegation and development opportunity.

HELPING ROLES

There are different roles that can help employees to be fully engaged in becoming their best: facilitator, coach and mentor.

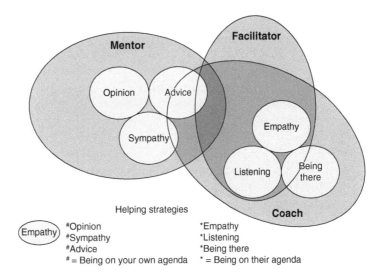

These styles pass accountability for their progression from the manager to the employee individually and as a team member. Helping others to become more effective is counter-intuitive in many instances; assisting, not commanding; helping, not controlling; encouraging and supporting rather than taking direct action; emphasizing employee responsibility rather than managerial accountability. Inexperienced managers may cling to the reverse of these behaviours. This is very different to outmoded behaviours such as coercive, autocratic and hierarchical management based on position and power.

We covered active listening skills in Chapter 6 and these are vital for any of the helping strategies. Equally, there is a lot of skill in challenging employees to develop targets, monitoring progress and measuring results. The relationship between a manager and the employee and related face-to-face meetings should contain:

▶ confidentiality
▶ constructive feedback
▶ creating space
▶ empathy
▶ genuineness
▶ managing silence
▶ observing skills
▶ open questioning
▶ referrals
▶ reflecting skills
▶ respect
▶ value systems.

In this example, the manager is adopting a coaching style of leadership to help an employee step up to the next grade in their profession.

Step 1 – Establish the contract. The conversation would include the following points.

▶ Coaching is a one-to-one personal development programme. Therefore, it is highly focused on your specific needs.
▶ The programme need not take you away from your job. We can use videoconferencing; it can be cost-effective.
▶ Define the challenge and describe the desired outcomes.
▶ The content needs to be based on your real-life issues so the outcomes have an immediate effect in the workplace and on your career.
▶ The programme is flexible and adaptable.
▶ The coaching relationship is based on mutual

understanding and respect so that the environment, though sometimes challenging, is safe and supportive.

▶ Both the coach and the employee will receive regular feedback.

▶ It can be transformational.

Step 2 – Define the barriers and hurdles which are impeding progress.

Step 3 – Brainstorm possible approaches.

Step 4 – Develop a C-SMART action plan in which goals are clearly defined.

Step 5 – Establish criteria for evaluation.

Step 6 – Facilitate action.

Step 7 – Follow through.

Managing the development of others

Record your thoughts and feelings regarding how you think you would be able to manage the tasks involved in developing others that are listed below. Be prepared to discuss the outcomes with your trusted adviser.

→ Confidentiality

_____

_____

→ Constructive feedback

_____

_____

→ Creating space for others

_____

_____

→ Empathy

_____

_____

→ Genuineness

_____

_____

→ Managing silence

_____

_____

→ Observing skills

_____

_____

→ Open questioning

_____

_____

→ Referrals

_____

_____

→ Reflecting skills

_____

_____

→ Respect

_____

_____

→ Shared value systems

_____

_____

Reflect on any past instances of trying to use these skills, noting any specific examples helpful to setting development targets.

_____

_____

_____

_____

Describe a better outcome of any critical incidents.

_____

_____

_____

_____

Note any present day implications or knock-on effects.

_____

_____

_____

_____

Developing others questionnaire

Using the legend as a guide, complete the questionnaire below. Tick a single response to each question according to how frequently you show that behaviour.

Grade	Legend and scoring instructions	Score
Always	There are no exceptions; you would have to think consciously about behaving any other way and changing what you do.	Add 4 points for every tick

Grade	Legend and scoring instructions	Score
Routinely	You would present yourself this way or react this way every week, with few exceptions.	Add 3 points for every tick
Sometimes	At your best, this is what you would be seen doing.	Add 2 points for every tick
Rarely	It would be considered unusual for this to be what you say, think or do.	Add 1 point for every tick
Never	There would be no exceptions; you do not present yourself this way to people at any time.	No points

Relationship management
People facilitating the development of capabilities in others

	Never (0)	Rarely (1)	Some-times (2)	Routinely (3)	Always (4)
Do you want to improve the performance of others?					
Can you identify gaps in the ability of others accurately?					
Can you deliver evidence-based feedback tactfully and effectively?					
Do you set reasonable expectations of performance for others?					
Do you recognize distinct results in others?					
Do you elicit and recall the aspirations of your employees?					

Relationship management
People facilitating the development of capabilities in others

	Never (0)	Rarely (1)	Some-times (2)	Routinely (3)	Always (4)
Do you have well-tuned listening skills which pick up performance issues?					
Can you delegate effectively to others?					
Do you bias feedback on negative performance issues?					
Are you authentic with people?					

We have encouraged you to develop a personal development plan. Identify what you need to add to your personal development plan to start demonstrating greater ability to develop others:

▶ the things that you do which breach trust or break rapport with employees

▶ the things that you need to do more often and do less often

▶ identify what is the cost of being weak at developing others.

Development needs

1 _____

_____

_____

_____

_____

_____

2 _____

_____

_____

_____

_____

_____

_____

_____

3 _____

_____

_____

_____

_____

_____

_____

_____

4 _____

_____

_____

_____

5 _____

→ Inspirational leadership

At the beginning of the chapter, we discussed employee engagement, authentic leadership and the helping roles involved in inspiring and developing employees. You will find there is much debate about leadership versus management, and many accepted theories about both. However, when you break it down to the fundamental benefit of hiring or promoting a person to a managerial role, it is to ensure that *other people* carry out tasks; the *right* work, being done *correctly* and *on time* for *valid* reasons, including profit. The role is not to increase the status of an individual, nor for them to do all the work themselves. An inspirational leader inspires individuals to work together effectively and efficiently on the right things to achieve planned goals.

Inspirational leaders build co-operation effectively, using hard information and individual needs to convince others to work towards a common purpose; they focus the whole group on a common vision and mission.

Good behaviours include:
- ▶ working interdependently with the group
- ▶ resolving disputes before they fester
- ▶ accepting sources of support
- ▶ persuading employees to buy in to the vision, mission and purpose
- ▶ using the facts in persuasion and bridging the gap between opposing sides
- ▶ breaking down barriers between those who work in their own little worlds without consulting each other.

Success in reaching organizational goals involves making the best use of all resources.

Identify with good role models, whether they are people that you have met or those you have identified in books, films or other places. Assess their strengths and your own. Be as diligent in reviewing and planning as you expect your employees to be. Make your own support environment as much a balance of challenge and genuine support as possible. Make sure that you too get enough praise for hard work, achievement and good practice as a leader to inspire you to greater heights.

Work with your peers and Human Resources department to make the climate at work as conducive as possible to good practice. Establish whatever change and communication mechanisms are appropriate and are easily accessible to the team; ask them to contribute ideas for improvement.

Review how effectively you have fulfilled your commitment to your team/division for the past month. What impact did this have on the climate within the team and on the team's performance? Strive to lead by example and to develop a climate of mutual respect and trust within the team.

People with the relationship management competence will have a considerable number of other emotional and social competencies at strength. They will be self-aware and have good self-control, be good at empathy and organizational awareness. It is likely that they have practised influencing and persuading capability. Combining these capabilities, they will be able to plan, organize, allocate and control, rallying a team of people towards an end goal. They will quickly divert team members from conflict and develop robust solutions and an agreed way ahead.

Inspirational leadership questionnaire

Using the legend as a guide, complete the questionnaire below. Tick a single response to each question according to how frequently you show that behaviour.

Grade	Legend and scoring instructions	Score
Always	There are no exceptions; you would have to think consciously about behaving any other way and changing what you do.	Add 4 points for every tick
Routinely	You would present yourself this way or react this way every week, with few exceptions.	Add 3 points for every tick
Sometimes	At your best, this is what you would be seen doing.	Add 2 points for every tick
Rarely	It would be considered unusual for this to be what you say, think or do.	Add 1 point for every tick
Never	There would be no exceptions; you do not present yourself this way to people at any time.	No points

Relationship management
Inspiring people towards delivery of a cohesive vision and mission

	Never (0)	Rarely (1)	Some-times (2)	Routinely (3)	Always (4)
Do you rally people to work together effectively?					
Do you defuse conflict and get a team back on track?					
Can you identify priority clashes and resolve them?					
Can you inspire team members in following a common vision?					
Do members of your team feel that they belong in the team?					

Relationship management
Inspiring people towards delivery of a cohesive vision and mission

	Never (0)	Rarely (1)	Some-times (2)	Routinely (3)	Always (4)
Do you empower individuals to set targets and monitor delivery?					
Do you inspire individuals to be at their best?					
Do you praise team members appropriately and accurately?					
Can you deal with mismatched allocation of resources?					
Do you represent your team with authority figures?					

We have encouraged you to develop a personal development plan. Ask yourself the following questions and then add to your personal development plan the things that you need to start doing to make your leadership more inspirational.

▶ Have you sufficient feedback to understand why others choose you as the leader?

▶ What things do you need to do more often, e.g. listening, one-to-one development sessions, remaining high-level rather than micromanaging?

▶ What is the cost of uninspiring leadership?

Summary

Developing your ability to manage others starts with your own capabilities in self-awareness and self-management. Next comes your awareness of others. Skill in each of these is essential if you are to manage other people successfully . But merely managing others is not really what we are concerned with here; to have credibility in this area of emotional intelligence, you will need to demonstrate:

▶ a strong ability to inspire others towards greater achievement

▶ active involvement in their development

▶ being a catalyst of change

▶ being a major influencer within your organization.

This is much more about leadership than management. So we looked at helping roles such as mentoring, facilitating and coaching and the strategies associated with them. We looked in some detail at the coaching process and specifically at your assessment of how you would be able to manage the tasks. You undertook a test of your disposition towards developing others; you also undertook an exercise in inspirational leadership.

The aim of this chapter was to help you to identify your own capability and motivation to lead, seeing yourself as others see you.

8 Becoming more resilient

In this chapter we look at resilience – what it is, why it is important and what we can do to improve it.

You will do some exercises to help you to:

▶ *identify your levels of resilience*
▶ *improve your resilience.*

WHAT IT IS

'*People who soar are those who refuse to sit back, sigh and wish things would change. They neither complain of their lot nor passively dream of some distant ship coming in. Rather, they visualize in their minds that they are not quitters; they will not allow life's circumstances to push them down and hold them under.*'

Charles Swindoll

Resilience is the quality that enables you to bounce back after encountering stressful, challenging or unsettling and often fast-paced events, to get back on the horse after falling off and resume your journey. The environment in which you operate today presents seemingly endless challenges and it is all too easy to buckle under the strain. It's your resilience that keeps you going, that helps you to tackle issues head-on and to come up smiling.

Your resilience is also dependent upon your cultural environment and background. For example, if as a child you had everything provided for you and were shielded from the harsher realities of life, then you may have reduced resilience. In your workplace, if you are strongly supported but face little challenge, you may have become complacent and have low levels of resilience when things change and become more challenging.

In the diagram below, which compares challenge and support, you can see that as you move or are required to move from a position of high support and low challenge to one of high support and high challenge, your *perception* is that the support you receive reduces as you transit the normal path (broken line) from one to the other. This is precisely when your resilience really matters.

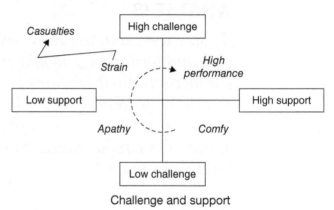

Challenge and support

Resilience is also about perspective. Different people react differently to different challenges, threats, stresses and adversity depending on their ability to cope, i.e. depending on their resilience. Resilience is fundamentally underpinned by the concept that it is not so much the hard times we face that determine our success or failure as the way in which we perceive those hard times.

→ Why resilience is important

It's generally accepted that resilience cannot be taught but it can be learned; it is learned through experience and practice. All of us have at some point or other in our lives come up against adversity. Those with high levels of resilience overcome such adversity; the challenges may set them back temporarily but they have the vision and determination to overcome them and move on. With low levels of resilience we shy away from really challenging circumstances so that we become risk avoiders; we do not stretch ourselves because we are more afraid of failure than we are driven by success; we become rooted within our comfort zone; we succumb to stress – in effect, we have ceased to live our lives. As a consequence, we do not reach our full potential; we resign ourselves to mediocrity; we accept second-best.

So, to be really alive, to live your life to the full, personally and at work, you need to develop high levels of resilience. But before you do that, you have to be aware of where you currently are on the resilience continuum. To find out, complete the following exercise designed to elicit your current levels of resilience.

→ Resilience traits

In her article 'How Resilience Works', Diane L. Coutu suggests that resilient individuals share three traits. You can think of a trait as being a relatively stable characteristic that causes individuals to behave in certain ways. These resilience traits are:

▶ a resolute acceptance of reality
▶ a sense that life is meaningful
▶ an exceptional ability to improvise.

Resilience traits questionnaire

Using the legend as a guide, evaluate your response to each statement. Mark your current position with an 'X' and your desired position with an 'O'. Then calculate the gap between your current and desired positions and enter this value in the gap column.

Grade	Legend and scoring instructions	Score
Always	There are no exceptions; you would have to think consciously about behaving any other way and changing what you do.	Add 4 points for every tick
Routinely	You would present yourself this way or react this way every week, with few exceptions.	Add 3 points for every tick
Sometimes	At your best, this is what you would be seen doing.	Add 2 points for every tick
Rarely	It would be considered unusual for this to be what you say, think or do.	Add 1 point for every tick
Never	There would be no exceptions; you do not present yourself this way to people at any time.	No points

Trait	Never (0)	Rarely (1)	Some-times (2)	Routinely (3)	Always (4)	Gap
I have a resolute acceptance of reality and put matters into perspective						
I have a strong sense that my life is meaningful and has direction						
I have an exceptional ability to improvise and find ways through issues						

Now record below where necessary what you will do to improve each of these traits to reach your desired levels.

→ I will improve my acceptance of reality by

_____

_____

_____

_____

→ I will improve the meaningfulness and direction of my life by

_____

_____

_____

_____

→ I will improve my ability to improvise and finds ways
through issues by

_____

_____

_____

_____

Now transfer these actions to your personal development
plan.

→ Ten ways to build resilience

The American Psychological Association suggests ten ways
to build resilience.

1 Maintain good relationships with close family members,
friends and others. This is your support network of
people who really know you and want you to succeed.
It's important to surround yourself with positive people
who themselves have high levels of resilience and self-
confidence. Think seriously about removing yourself
from the influence of people who 'drain' you or 'put you
down'.

2 Avoid seeing crises or stressful events as unbearable
problems. This is about putting things into proper
perspective and then finding ways to work through
the issues. The process may involve some degree of
compromise but you will find that you develop a more
positive mental attitude.

3 Accept circumstances that cannot be changed. There are
many things over which we have little or no control. It's
wasteful of your time and energy to try to change the

unchangeable. It's much better to accept the situation and move on.

4 Develop realistic goals and move towards them (see Chapter 5). Remember to set C-SMART goals and to review them regularly to make sure that they remain relevant and that you are on track.

5 Take decisive actions in adverse situations. This is very important; there is no room for prevarication in adverse situations. If you fail to take urgent action, the issue will almost certainly get worse and take considerably more effort to resolve. If you have a number of issues, prioritize them by ranking them according to the combination of their urgency and importance, acting first on those that are both urgent *and* important.

6 Look for opportunities for self-discovery after a struggle with loss. Loss manifests in many ways, e.g. bereavement, loss of self-confidence, loss of a job, loss of something cherished. While the depth of loss that you feel will depend on the circumstances, there is a predictable path that many will follow to some degree or other. See the section on the Kübler-Ross change curve below.

7 Developing self-confidence. You looked at self-confidence as part of your self-motivation in Chapter 6, especially with regard to the negative-belief cycle. Take this further by completing the Five Whys exercise below.

8 Keep a long-term perspective and consider any stressful event in a broader context. This aspect of resilience is covered in a number of places in this workbook, including the negative-belief cycle in Chapter 6 and the Kübler-Ross change curve section and the Five Whys exercise below.

9   Maintain a hopeful outlook, expecting good things and visualizing what is wished for. Once again, this is about your positive mental attitude, setting and achieving your goals and developing your self-confidence. Visualization can be a powerful way of reframing old issues into new ways forward. Just attach a positive mental picture to the old issue.

10 Take care of your mind and body, exercising regularly, paying attention to your own needs and feelings and engaging in relaxing activities that you enjoy. We all recognize that when we feel good, we are good, we perform well. Give yourself the tender, loving care that you deserve.

→ The Kübler-Ross change curve

Dr Elisabeth Kübler-Ross developed the grief cycle as part of her work in the support and counselling of personal trauma, grief and grieving associated with death and dying. However, it is now widely accepted that similar reactions are found in people confronted with far less serious traumas, such as redundancy, enforced relocation, crime and punishment, disability and injury, relationship break-up, financial difficulties and bankruptcy. The model is therefore often referred to as 'the change curve'.

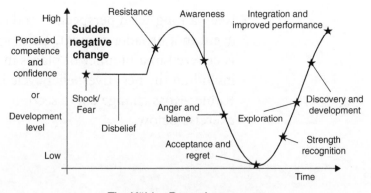

The Kübler-Ross change curve

Just being aware of these classic reactions to a loss situation can be empowering in itself. You should be aware that different people react with different intensities, not everyone will experience the full range of emotions, and some people will transition through the curve faster than others, while others may become stuck or delayed at different stages.

The change curve

Think of an instance when you experienced a significant change or loss. Record the circumstances and then describe how you transitioned along the curve. Then describe how you moved on from the change or loss. Finally, state how you could apply this experience to future loss/change situations.

→ Record the circumstances of the loss

_____

_____

_____

_____

_____

_____

→ How I moved along the change curve

_____

_____

_____

_____

_____

_____

→How I moved on from the change or loss

_____

_____

_____

_____

_____

→How I could apply this experience to future loss/change situations

_____

_____

_____

_____

_____

_____

_____

→ Developing self-confidence

Sometimes it's quite difficult to get to the root cause of some of your personal issues. Here's a way to help that process.

Think of an issue that needs to be resolved. State the issue in terms of its negative impact, e.g. when my best friend expresses an opinion with which I don't agree, I never challenge her. Now ask yourself *why* you never challenge her. Repeat the process in the context of your response to each 'why' five times. The process could progress something like this:

When my best friend expresses an opinion with which I don't agree, I never challenge it.

Why not? Because I am afraid to upset her.

Why are you afraid of the possibility of upsetting her? Because it can make people angry.

Why should that make you afraid? Because I remember an incident from the past when I upset someone and the repercussions were immense.

Why should a bad experience from the past necessarily be a bad experience today? Because that's the way things are.

Why are things that way? Because I make them that way by not being sufficiently self-confident to be assertive with people.

That's right, you make them that way through a story you've written around a bad experience. You apply that story to all similar occurrences. Does that make sense in your adult world today? No.

By applying this process of deconstruction to your unwanted issues, you can find the trigger for the issue. You can then build a new pathway in your brain for your new desired outcome and stop following the old pathway. That is a process of applying your internal observer to nurture rather than criticize yourself. As a result, you become more self-confident – and more resilient.

The Five Whys

Now complete the exercise with an issue of your own.

→ Describe the issue.

_____

_____

_____

_____

→ First *Why* and outcome

_____

_____

_____

_____

→ Second *Why* and outcome

_____

_____

_____

_____

→ Third *Why* and outcome

_____

_____

_____

_____

→ Fourth *Why* and outcome

_____

_____

_____

_____

→ Fifth *Why* and outcome

_____

_____

_____

_____

Have you arrived at the original trigger of the ultimate outcome? You will know if you have because usually it feels emotionally uncomfortable.

You may not need to ask 'why?' five times; you may reach the trigger more quickly. Or you may need to keep going until you feel sure that you have got to the real trigger.

Now describe the new positive pathway.

_____

_____

_____

_____

When [the old trigger] arises, I will recognize it as

_____

_____

_____

_____

And take the following action

_____

_____

_____

_____

Summary

In this chapter we defined resilience as the ability to bounce back after a challenging situation. You saw that your resilience depends upon your physical and cultural environment and background, on how much you are supported through life and by your perspective of the world around you.

You discovered the resilience traits of:

▶ a resolute acceptance of reality

▶ a sense that life is meaningful

▶ an exceptional ability to improvise.

You then undertook exercises to establish:

▶ what you will do to improve each of these resilience traits to reach your desired levels

▶ how you can better handle change by understanding the change curve

▶ how to get to the root cause of issues you face and how to put them into perspective

You were also given ten ways to build your resilience.

9 Developing your influencing skills

In this chapter we look at developing influencing skills – what they are, why they are important and what we can do to improve them. We look at three aspects of influencing:

▶ *skills*
▶ *styles*
▶ *strategies.*

You will also do some exercises to help you to:

▶ *identify your current levels of influencing skills*
▶ *improve your influencing skills.*

WHAT IT IS

'Because everything we say and do is the length and shadow of our own souls, our influence is determined by the quality of our being.'

Dale E. Turner

Influence is defined as the capacity or power of persons or things to be a compelling force on or to produce effects on the actions, behaviour, opinions, etc., of others.

→ Why influencing skills are important

Influencing skills affect us every day in every situation, whether consciously or subconsciously. Subconsciously, your very presence exerts influence in one way or another on the people and situations that surround you; you can label this form of influence as 'covert'. You'll recognize that you need to ensure these influences are 'good', that they support and enhance your position in your world. The emotional intelligence skills you are developing (self-awareness, self-control, awareness of others, management of others) will directly support your covert influencing.

The conscious or 'overt' form of influencing occurs when you actively seek to exert influence on other people and situations by taking some sort of action. This form of influence takes place in meetings, presentations, debates, discussions and the like. These influencing skills are different and are needed in addition to your covert skills; the covert skills are required since you have to establish a relationship with the other people involved, so your way of being needs to be supportive, not a hindrance.

Influencing skills in others

Think about someone you have admired for their ability to influence others. What soft skills (the sort of person they are) and hard skills (techniques) did they demonstrate? Make a note of these below; we've given you some to get you started.

Soft influencing skills	Hard influencing skills
Active listening/Quickly establishes rapport	*Knows what he wants/Knows what she's prepared to sacrifice*

Well done for completing the first exercise. In case you missed some of the skills, there's a comprehensive list below of the hard skills required for successful influencing.

There's no definitive list of influencing skills, but what follows will stand you in good stead.

Planning. When you are embarking on a specific need to influence someone towards a desired result, you need to plan the process carefully.

▶ The physical environment must be conducive to the occasion.

▶ You must know exactly what your desired outcome is.

▶ You must know what you are prepared to trade and not trade away. Look for a balance; when you concede something, expect something back in return.

▶ You must know what your bottom line is and not cross it.

▶ You must try to work out what the other party will object to and how you will handle these objections. 'Stand in their shoes' to try to see things from their perspective.

▶ You must recognize that the other party will be undertaking a similar planning process.

▶ You must try to achieve a win/win end result. If you don't, it's likely that any agreement will subsequently collapse.

Self-awareness. You will deploy your self-awareness skills, part of which is knowing exactly when any of your 'hot buttons' are pressed.

Self-control. You'll be better able to manage your own reactions to what's going on, especially if any of your 'hot buttons' are pressed.

Awareness of others. This skill gives you insight into how others are feeling and behaving so that you are better able to manage them.

Management of others. Your skills in the management of others are essential in any overt influencing event.

Establishing rapport. Your emotional intelligence skills enable you to establish the essential rapport quickly and convincingly so that you win people over. What attracts others towards you and therefore towards what you want is your way of being.

Probing and questioning. Skilful probing and questioning from broad questions funnelling down to more detailed exploration of issues is essential. It goes hand in hand with the next skill – active listening.

Active listening. By demonstrating active listening, you indicate to the other party that you are interested in them and what they have to say. You can demonstrate active listening by:

- making regular eye contact
- leaning forward towards them
- nodding your head in agreement or shaking your head in disagreement
- repeating back some of their words and terminology
- making noises of agreement
- using other supportive body language
- not interrupting.

Persuasive dialogue. Being persuasive means that:

- you've done your research and have your arguments clearly fashioned
- you acknowledge the other party's right to their opinions and positions, just as you have those rights too
- you remain calm and courteous at all times but do not allow the other party to dominate you
- you allow equal time for each party to put their case
- you are able to summarize accurately and convincingly.

Assertiveness. Everyone has the right to be listened to and for their opinions to be acknowledged. No one has the right to discount you or your views. Being assertive is about being very clear and focused about what you want to happen. Try the following assertive approach whenever you feel you are not being given a fair hearing.

- Describe the situation as you currently see it.
- Describe how that situation makes you feel. What emotions does it cause in you?
- Describe in some detail what outcome you would like to happen.
- Describe the impact that outcome would have on you.
- Describe the impact that outcome would have on the other party.
- Ask for the other party's agreement.

Flexibility/adaptability. In seeking to influence others positively, it's important to remain flexible and adaptable. No one likes someone who digs their heels in and won't budge, or who is closed to new ideas and new ways.

My influencing skills gaps

Complete the following exercise to determine the gaps between where you are now and where you want to be in terms of your influencing skills.

Score each of the following influencing skills from 0 (low) to 5 (five), first as you currently rate yourself and then as you would like to be rated. Then establish the gap between the two.

Influencing skills	Current score	Desired score	Gap
Planning			
Self-awareness			
Self-control			
Awareness of others			
Management of others			
Establishing rapport			
Probing and questioning			
Active listening			
Persuasive dialogue			
Assertiveness			
Flexibility/adaptability			

Using the gap as a guide, sort the influencing skills into priority order, with the first being the largest gap, and so on. Then describe what you could do to improve the skill and by when.

Influencing skills in order of priority	What I could do	By date
1.		
2.		
3.		
4.		
5.		
6.		

7.		
8.		
9.		
10.		
11.		

Extract your actions and the dates by which they should be completed into your personal development plan.

Let's bring influencing skills closer to home by looking at specific situations at work and in your personal life through the following exercise.

My influencing skills

Think about your day-to-day role(s) at work and a normal day in your personal life. Make a list of the situations in which you think you need or want to influence others:

→ Work situations

_____

_____

_____

_____

_____

_____

_____

_____

_____

_____

_____

_____

→ Personal situations

_____

_____

_____

_____

_____

_____

_____

_____

_____

_____

_____

Select the most important three from your work list, and make a note of anything you find difficult about influencing people in those situations. Then, using all you have learnt so far in this workbook, describe what you could do to improve your influencing capabilities.

My difficulty at work	What I will do to resolve it
Situation 1	
Situation 2	
Situation 3	

Repeat the exercise for the top three issues in your personal life.

My difficulty in my personal life	What I will do to resolve it
Situation 1	
Situation 2	
Situation 3	

It's worth repeating again here that your emotional intelligence competencies within self-awareness, self-control, awareness of others and management of others are key covert influencing skills.

→ Influencing styles

In addition to influencing skills, we need to explore influencing styles, i.e. the different ways we can approach influencing events.

Most people have one preferred style of influencing behaviour but this may not always be appropriate to the situation. It's wise to develop a number of styles so that you can adapt your style to the prevailing circumstances.

Influencing styles are the sets of behaviours which have a particular impact on the person you are trying to influence.

There are many different views on influencing styles but you can consider them as four styles, each with their own associated behaviours. These four styles fit within two categories, Productive and Unproductive:

Productive	Unproductive
Assertive (I win)	Aggressive (You lose)
Responsive (You win)	Passive (I lose)

Their associated behaviours are:

Productive		Unproductive	
Assertive (I win)	Responsive (We win)	Aggressive (You lose)	Passive (I lose)
Expressing want	Active listening/ enquiring	Interrogating	Accommodating
Rewards and penalties	Expressing positive regard and support	Patronizing	Self put-downs
Giving feedback	Disclosure	Showing contempt	Self-pitying
Logical expression	Finding common ground	Attacking	Avoiding
	Visioning		

Of these styles, the most productive is the responsive style because it's aiming for a win/win outcome. Sometimes, you may need to use the assertive or the aggressive styles when you have to get the outcome you want. Both of these styles are referred to as 'push' styles as you are pushing your arguments onto the other party. The responsive style is a 'pull' style because you are pulling information from the other party to support the outcome. 'Pull' helps to create the win/win outcome.

Only productive behaviours will be appropriate in long-term, positive-influence relationships. Unproductive behaviours will not achieve your desired outcomes and the aggressive style will make enemies. You need to know about these styles so that you can handle them when they arise.

In all influencing situations, establishing long-term relationships is key. You cannot realistically expect to achieve productive outcomes if you do not invest in your relationships.

My default (preferred) influencing style

Guided by the definitions of these four influencing styles, describe your preferred style.

→ My preferred influencing style is characterized by these behaviours

_____

_____

_____

_____

_____

_____

➔ So my preferred influencing style is

_____

Now decide which of the other styles you wish to add to your influencing styles inventory and describe how you would approach using these styles.

➔ My second influencing style would be

_____

➔ My approach would be

_____

_____

_____

_____

➔ My third influencing style would be

_____

➔ My approach would be

_____

_____

_____

_____

→ Influencing strategies

There are seven distinctive influencing strategies. However, the line between each strategy is cut and dried. While you might have a preferred strategy at the centre of your approach, you will undoubtedly need to employ different strategies for different situations or even for different people in the same situation.

All productive influence strategies require the use of the assertive and responsive influence styles. The diagram below illustrates the continuum where the strategies lie relative to the behaviours associated with assertive and responsive influence styles.

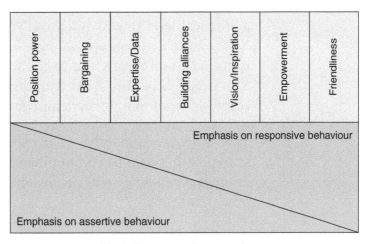

The influence strategy continuum

It will be helpful to look at these strategies individually.

Friendliness. This involves showing warmth and positive feelings towards others and generally acting in a friendly and supportive way towards them. It builds trust and rapport so that others will accept your ideas and wish to co-operate with you. It is especially useful when trust, openness and a strong personal relationship are required. However, it takes time to build such relationships.

Empowerment. This has two key elements:

► providing a clear and appropriate overall direction for others without controlling the detail of what they need to do or how they should do it

► showing confidence and trust in others' capabilities, listening to them without taking away their responsibility, and showing empathy.

This is most likely to be relevant, but not exclusive, to those with a leadership role, to encourage those they are leading to take more responsibility. It demands time and commitment.

Vision/Inspiration. The key here is to develop a shared vision which appeals strongly at both an emotional and a practical level to you *and* those you wish to influence. You need to demonstrate genuine interest and enthusiasm for others' aspirations and to connect these to your own. This needs to be combined with displaying a genuine and constant belief that positive outcomes can be achieved.

This strategy is adaptable to any situation where long-term shared enthusiasm or commitment is required. However, at times it can be seen as insubstantial unless backed up by other strategies.

Building alliances. This involves finding common interests with others who are in a position to support your influencing efforts. This could be on a specific issue or something major that you want to achieve. To be successful, you need to be able to:

► identify and make contact with potential allies

► find common interests

► develop a clear understanding of how mutual support can be obtained.

This strategy comes into its own when you cannot achieve your influence objective without support. Otherwise, you may be making unnecessary commitments.

Expertise/Data. This strategy depends on using data and expert opinion to reinforce what you want to achieve. To be effective in your strategy, your evidence needs to be substantial and your proposals targeted at those you want to influence. Sometimes this strategy requires you to increase your own levels of experience or to supplement them with other experts.

This is a popular strategy because logic and data are strong currencies in most organizations. It can run into difficulties when resistance is at the level of emotions or values.

Bargaining. This involves making deals to secure others' support for you. You need to understand what others' needs are and to have relevant incentives (possibly pressures) to apply. You must also be an effective negotiator. Bargaining is a good fall-back strategy when others need to be supported. It can be especially effective for securing support or neutralizing opposition on specific issues. Its limitation is that the backing usually only lasts as long as the associated incentives or pressures.

Position power. Position power and personal power are dealt with in more detail in Chapter 12. Position power involves using your position in a hierarchy to influence others. You must be seen to have a legitimate right through your role to demand or request the response that you require. The style and circumstances for using this strategy will be crucial in determining whether it is perceived as positive or negative. This style can be useful for making things happen quickly, particularly when your need to influence is acute. However, it almost invariably results in compliance, not commitment, unless strongly supported by another strategy.

Summary

In this chapter you have looked at the concept of influencing with particular emphases on:

Influencing skills

- ▶ Planning
- ▶ Self awareness
- ▶ Self-control
- ▶ Awareness of others
- ▶ Management of others
- ▶ Establishing rapport
- ▶ Probing and questioning
- ▶ Active listening
- ▶ Persuasive dialogue
- ▶ Assertiveness
- ▶ Flexibility/adaptability

Influencing styles

- ▶ Productive
  - ▷ Assertive
  - ▷ Responsive
- ▶ Unproductive
  - ▷ Aggressive
  - ▷ Passive

Influencing strategies

- ▶ Friendliness
- ▶ Empowerment
- ▶ Vision/Inspiration
- ▶ Building alliances
- ▶ Expertise/Data
- ▶ Bargaining

▶ Position power

The exercises you have undertaken have been designed to help you to:

▶ recognize the influencing skills that others use

▶ determine the influencing gaps in your toolbox and how you can close them

▶ look at how you can tackle a current influencing issue at work and in your personal life

▶ determine your preferred influencing style and how you can develop others.

10 Conflict resolution

In this chapter we look at conflict resolution, which may become necessary during an influencing process. We explore Thomas and Kilmann's theory of conflict resolution and the associated styles. We also look at the interest-based relational (IBR) approach to conflict resolution, followed by an examination of the nine-stage process of conflict resolution.

Exercises covering your experience of conflict resolution, your preferred conflict resolution style, how you managed a conflict, your behaviours during conflict, barriers to conflict resolution and how you applied hindsight, mid-sight and foresight to a conflict situation will help you to cement your learning.

WHAT IT IS

'Conflict is inevitable, but combat is optional.'

Max Lucade

A commonly applied definition of conflict is 'a disagreement through which the parties involved perceive a threat to their needs, interests or concerns'. There are several words within this definition which merit closer attention.

'Disagreement' is a relatively benign word, but here it is qualified by the more robust term 'threat'. A threat can be physical or emotional, real or implied, and is a challenge to our well-being, status or way of life. A threat is invariably taken seriously, and it and its implications need to be resolved before it can be dismissed.

The word 'perceive' is also important. We know very well that different people perceive different events in different ways and that they react to them in different ways. So what is a minor threat to one person may be a major threat to another. Think back to Maslow's hierarchy of needs in Chapter 5 and consider how your position in the hierarchy might change your perception of a threat to you.

As the first quotation above states, conflict is common; it's all around us. But its existence does not mean that we have to engage in a war to overcome it. Combat or war should be last resorts when other approaches have failed.

There are many forms of conflict resolution, the most common of which are probably:

▶ influencing, through:
  ▷ negotiation, in which both sides discuss the issue to find a way through
  ▷ mediation, in which a third party seeks to assist the parties in dispute to find a resolution but is unable to enforce the resolution
  ▷ arbitration, in which a third party assists the parties in dispute to find a resolution and has the power to decide on the form of the resolution
▶ use of force, which is extremely aggressive, has limited long-term success and can quickly back-fire and escalate a conflict.

The influencing approaches require the deployment of your emotional intelligence skills: self-awareness, self-control, awareness of others and management of others. You will see right away that the first two manage your physical and emotional reactions to an external threat of conflict, while the last two enable you to take the heat out of a conflict situation driven by someone else.

My experience of conflict resolution

Most of us have been involved at some point in conflict and having to find a resolution. Think back to a past experience of such an incident at work or in your private life and describe the situation and who was involved. Then note what action was taken by the parties involved, how the process felt, what the outcome was and how this impacted on each of the parties in dispute.

→ Describe the situation and who was involved.

_____

_____

_____

_____

→ What action was taken?

_____

_____

_____

_____

→ How did the process feel?

_____

_____

→ What was the outcome?

_____

_____

_____

→ Describe the impact on each of the parties involved.

_____

_____

_____

_____

→ What were the lessons you learned about conflict resolution?

_____

_____

_____

_____

→ Why conflict resolution is important

You know that conflict is inevitable. What really matters is how it's handled. If it's dealt with in an adult and mature way, with each party respecting the other's needs and their position and understanding the benefits of finding a way through, then conflict can present opportunities. On the other hand, throwing your toys out of the pram and reacting angrily to a conflict situation can sometimes place the other party at an advantage and certainly brings your own position into bad focus. Nor is avoidance a healthy strategy, as the issue will fester and grow. Also, conflict engenders strong emotions which over time can lead to stress and illness. Finally, conflict situations often lead to over-reactions and become self-fulfilling prophesies. What's more important: restoring happy and healthy relationships or those relationships falling apart? You know the answer.

There are other benefits. As well as bringing conflict to an end, conflict resolution can also bring about enduring changes in relationships, increased understanding, greater cohesion and better self-understanding.

→ Conflict styles

In the 1970s, Kenneth Thomas and Ralph Kilmann developed a theory of conflict resolution centred on five main styles, each of which depends on degrees of co-operation and assertiveness. As with influencing styles, you will have a preferred style but you should also be able to call on other styles which are driven by the circumstances of the conflict situation.

The five recognized styles Thomas and Kilmann identified are:
- competitive
- collaborative
- compromising
- accommodating
- avoiding.

You should be able to characterize these from your study of this workbook so far.

Now let's check your understanding of the styles by looking at them in more detail.

Competitive. In this often power-based style, you push (see Chapter 9) your own needs and desired outcome to the detriment of the other party's needs and wants. The style is often aggressive and controlling, has little regard for future relationships and can result in escalating levels of threat. There is little or no trust associated with this style. It has a strongly negative impact on the other party.

Collaborative. In this style the approach seeks to achieve a win/win outcome based on a common goal. Assertive behaviour is often associated with it and shared ideas and expanding views of possibilities characterize this style. It is based on trust, and often brings about outcomes which exceed the original desired outcome. It has a strongly positive impact.

Compromising. This style is based on give and take, on trade-offs. It is a middle-ground style which seeks to avoid risk while to some extent pleasing everyone. There is some lack of trust and the impact is on the positive side of neutral.

Accommodating. In this style, preserving the relationship is more important than achieving a desired outcome, so needs and wants are yielded. Some might see this style as diplomatic, but it is not; it is sacrificial and one-dimensional. It reduces the respect which the other party should hold of you. It lies on the negative side of neutral.

Avoiding. This style is characterized by a head-in-the-sand attitude, the hope that 'if we ignore it, it will go away'. Instead, the issue festers and grows out of all proportion to its initial impact; consequently it becomes more and more difficult to resolve. In the end it explodes, killing trust and destroying relationships. It has huge negative impact.

My preferred conflict resolution style

From your understanding of the five conflict resolution styles, complete the questionnaire below. Against each style, score yourself according to how often you use that style; 'Never' scores 0 and 'Always' scores 4. Then enter the row score in the right-hand column to determine your preferred style.

Preferred style	Never (0)	Rarely (1)	Some-times (2)	Routinely (3)	Always (4)	Score
Competitive						
Collaborative						
Compromising						
Accommodating						
Avoiding						

My preferred style is:

_____

Let's now look at your historical reaction to conflict.

How I could have managed a conflict better

Think about a recent conflict. Choose a different one from that used in the exercise 'My experience of conflict resolution'.

→ Describe the situation.

_____

_____

_____

_____

_____

→ The style I used.

_____

_____

_____

_____

→ Describe the outcome.

_____

_____

_____

_____

_____

_____

→ Was the outcome what you wanted?

_____

_____

_____

_____

_____

→ What style would have been more appropriate?

_____

_____

_____

_____

_____

_____

My behaviours

Thinking about the same event as in the previous exercise, describe how you perceived the conflict, how you behaved and which emotional intelligence skills you did or didn't apply and why.

→ How I perceived the conflict and whether my
   perceptions clouded the issue

_____

_____

_____

_____

_____

→ How I behaved during the conflict

_____

_____

_____

_____

_____

→ How I behaved during the resolution process

_____

_____

_____

_____

_____

_____

➜ The emotional intelligence skills I used and why

_____

_____

_____

_____

_____

➜ The emotional intelligence skills I did not use and why

_____

_____

_____

_____

_____

What have you learned from this exercise? How robust
are your emotional intelligence skills?

....

THE INTEREST-BASED RELATIONAL APPROACH

Another concept of conflict resolution is the interest-based relational (IRB) approach. This frequently used approach is based on respecting individuals' interests and differences while avoiding becoming bogged down in fixed positions. The approach is governed by the following rules.

▶ **Good relationships are the first priority.** Take great care to ensure that you try to build mutual respect, act courteously, and remain calm and constructive.

▶ **Separate people and problems.** People have the right to be heard and to put their case without being judged or stereotyped. By separating the issue from the personality, you can maintain relationships and concentrate on the issue.

▶ **Listen actively** (see Chapter 4) so that you gain a clear understanding of the other's position. If you don't understand, seek clarification.

▶ **Use your ears first and mouth second.** This follows on from active listening. Really listen and understand, avoid interrupting, and have your say when the time is appropriate.

▶ **Fact, not fiction.** Stick to the facts of the situation and avoid emotional associations and hijacks (see Chapter 2). Stick to an agreed process and avoid surprises.

▶ **Work together.** When it comes to resolving problems, two brains are better than one. Bounce ideas off one another, and be open to new ideas and ways of thinking rather than being stuck on a predetermined solution.

If you follow these rules, you will improve the probability of reaching a mutually beneficial resolution to conflict.

→ The process of conflict resolution

The styles and behaviours that will help to resolve conflict can be brought together to form a process.

Stage 1: Gain agreement for the process to be followed. As a general rule, you should try to follow this process. There will be occasions when you can't because the other party won't let you; at this point try to convince them otherwise, but if they won't play along, take part yourself while making it clear that your overriding aim is to sort the issue out.

Stage 2: Try to identify the default style. If you've worked together before to resolve conflict, what style was used? When you understand what style the other party is likely to employ, you can react appropriately to it.

Stage 3: Set the scene. This is your opportunity to adopt the IBR approach, explaining how you intend to conduct yourself to the other party. Ask them to adopt a similar approach, if necessary explaining why this might be better than a negative style.

Stage 4: Get to the root of the issue. Explore the interests, needs, wants and concerns of both parties; remember the Five Whys (Chapter 8). What is the impact of the issue? Make sure you ignore the personalities involved.

Stage 5: Agree what the problem is. While this may sound obvious, this stage is about bringing both sides' perceptions into the open and conducting a reality check. Try to gain agreement on what the issue is, but if you can't, at least acknowledge the different views.

Stage 6: Initiate a process of problem-solving. This might include brainstorming, force-field analysis, SWOT (strengths/weaknesses/opportunities/threats) analysis, PEST/PESTLE (political, economic, sociological, technological, legal, environmental) analysis, etc. Make sure that both parties are happy with the selected process.

Stage 7: Negotiate the solution. Now that you have all the data in place and have analysed the situation, you should have enough information to arrive at a solution. It may be necessary to negotiate around the detail (see Chapter 9) so you should aim for a win/win outcome.

Stage 8: Sell the solution. Now you need to sell the solution to anyone else who is part of the problem. Again, your influencing skills come into play.

Stage 9: Celebrate success. Congratulations on getting to an agreed and mutually beneficial solution. Both parties should celebrate the success.

Barriers to conflict resolution

Think about the barriers that might get in the way of successful conflict resolution. Make a list in the box below of those that you have come across.

→ Barriers I have come across.

_____

_____

_____

_____

_____

_____

→ Now make a list of any others you can think of as a result of studying this chapter.

_____

_____

_____

_____

_____

_____

→ Describe how you would overcome them.

_____

_____

_____

_____

_____

_____

Check your list against the one below. This list is not comprehensive but it does includes many of the barriers you are likely to encounter:

► clashes of communication styles
► cultural
► emotions (pent-up frustration and anger, embarrassment, defensiveness)
► hidden agendas
► historic – social conditioning, prejudice and other filters
► lack of confidence
► loss of focus/attention

▶ mismatched styles

▶ misunderstanding of the process being applied by both parties

▶ not-invented-here attitude

▶ terminology and vocabulary.

Hindsight, mid-sight and foresight

Chapter 2 provided you with an understanding of hindsight, mid-sight and foresight. Think now of a conflict situation, and describe below what impact applying each of these might have had.

→ The situation

_____

_____

_____

_____

_____

→ The impact of applying hindsight

_____

_____

_____

_____

_____

_____

→ The impact of applying mid-sight

_____

_____

_____

_____

_____

_____

→ The impact of applying foresight

_____

_____

_____

_____

_____

_____

Summary

In this chapter, we have looked at your experience of conflict resolution and why it's important. We examined Thomas and Kilmann's theory of conflict resolution centred on five main styles: competitive; collaborative; compromising; accommodating; avoiding.

Then we looked at your behaviours during conflict situations before examining the interest-based relational (IBR) approach to conflict resolution:

▶ good relationships are the first priority

▶ separate people and problems

▶ listen actively

▶ use your ears first and mouth second

▶ fact, not fiction

▶ work together.

We followed this with a look at the nine-stage process of conflict resolution:

1 Gain agreement for the process to be followed

2 Try to identify the default style

3 Set the scene

4 Get to the root of the issue

5 Agree what the problem is

6 Initiate a process of problem solving

7 Negotiate the solution

8 Sell the solution

9 Celebrate success.

This chapter closed with exercises on barriers to conflict resolution and hindsight, mid-sight and foresight.

11 Achievement orientation

In this chapter we look at your achievement orientation, your drive to excel in what you do, to go the extra mile and to outperform others by taking positive action. We look at the characteristics or achievement orientation and why it's important. We also examine the impact of the way you've been living your life on your successes and disappointments.

You will do some exercises to help you to:

▶ *determine your current levels of achievement orientation*

▶ *improve your achievement orientation.*

WHAT IT IS

'My dreams are worthless, my plans are dust, my goals are impossible. All are of no value unless they are followed by action.'

Og Mandino

Achievement orientation is the drive you feel to excel in what you do, to go the extra mile and to outperform others by taking positive action. But it is not just about accomplishing a task; it goes well beyond that. It's about a strongly held personal desire to succeed through your own efforts, to carry on when others fall by the wayside, and to reach peak performance despite the barriers that may get in your way. It is strongly allied to your self-motivation (see Chapter 5) and your resilience (see Chapter 8). It requires clear focus, setting and achieving challenging goals (Chapter 5), a powerful vision of what you want your future to look like, and a relentless drive to get there and beyond.

One view of achievement orientation comes from Daniel Coleman, who popularized the concept of emotional intelligence in the 1990s. People with this competence:

▶ are results-oriented, with a high drive to meet their objectives and standards

▶ set challenging goals and take calculated risks

▶ pursue information to reduce uncertainty and find ways to do better

▶ learn how to improve their performance.

→ Why achievement orientation is important

Achievement orientation is important on two levels: on a personal level for your self-esteem and well-being; in your personal and working relationships for a happy and successful life. Ultimately, achievement orientation is about being successful. Different people view success in different ways so it's important that you define what success looks like and feels like to you. It's also important to have mini-successes on the way towards achieving your big dream.

My achievement orientation questionnaire

Complete the questionnaire below. Against each of the competencies, tick a single response to each question according to how frequently you show that behaviour; 'Never' scores 0 and 'Always' scores 4. Then add up your column scores to give your total score.

Grade	Legend and scoring instructions	Score
Always	There are no exceptions; you would have to think consciously about behaving any other way and changing what you do.	Add 4 points for every tick
Routinely	You would present yourself this way or react this way every week, with few exceptions.	Add 3 points for every tick
Some-times	At your best, this is what you would be seen doing.	Add 2 points for every tick
Rarely	It would be considered unusual for this to be what you say, think or do.	Add 1 point for every tick
Never	There would be no exceptions; you do not present yourself this way to people at any time.	No points

Statement	Never (0)	Rarely (1)	Sometimes (2)	Routinely (3)	Always (4)
I believe in myself					
I am clear about what success looks like to me					
I have a clear vision of my future					
I set challenging goals aligned to my vision					
I take positive action to achieve my goals and am results orientated					
I take risks					
I am resilient					
I am open to new ideas and ways of being					
I commit fully and do not quit					
I have a strong support network					
I identify and analyse problems and provide solutions					
I hold myself and others accountable for their areas of responsibility					
I exercise good judgement and make sound decisions					
I enjoy my journey to success					
Column score					
Total score					

Now check the feedback on your score.

Score = 43–56. Congratulations, you have a high to exceptional achievement orientation, with a positive vision of your future. You set clear goals aligned to that vision and are determined to achieve them.

Actions to take: With well-developed achievement orientation you may choose to help others in your circle of influence. Doing so will benefit them and you will also gain from the interactions.

Score = 29–42. Well done, you should be pleased with the results. You would benefit from further developing your achievement orientation to maximize the success you clearly want to achieve.

Actions to take: Complete this chapter, especially the exercises it contains. You could also seek out someone you admire for their achievement orientation and ask for their support in improving your own.

Score = 15–28. Well done for completing this exercise. You can certainly take action to improve your achievement orientation if you choose to do so. Some people are satisfied with their lives and their successes and do not wish to progress further; others are keen to move forward.

Actions to take: Complete this chapter, especially the exercises it contains. You could also seek out someone you admire for their achievement orientation and ask for their support in improving your own. In addition, you may wish to embark on a personal development course or a coaching programme which would help you to improve your achievement orientation and, ultimately, your personal success.

Score = 1–14. Thank you for being so honest. Showing integrity is a great emotional intelligence strength. There is much you can do to improve your achievement orientation, and doing so is likely to bring greater success in both your personal and working lives.

Actions to take: If you are happy with your current levels of success, then you may decide that you do not wish to pursue this skill further. However, you would benefit greatly from continuing with this chapter and perhaps revisiting previous chapters as this book has been gradually building your skills towards achieving greater success in your life. In addition, you may wish to embark on a personal development course or a coaching programme which would help you to improve your achievement orientation and, ultimately, your personal success.

→ Developing achievement orientation

Let's move on to see how you can develop greater achievement orientation.

Could do better

Think of a time when you felt that you could have done better in some challenging environment, either at work or in your personal life. Describe the situation and then why things did not work out as well as you wanted them to. Where appropriate, relate the reasons to the factors in the questionnaire in the previous exercise.

→ Describe the situation

_____

_____

_____

_____

_____

_____

→ Why things didn't go well

_____

_____

_____

_____

_____

Could do worse

Think of a time when you felt that you could have done worse in some challenging environment, either at work or in your personal life. Describe the situation and then why things worked out well. Where appropriate, relate the reasons to the factors in the exercise 'My achievement orientation' questionnaire.

→ Describe the situation

_____

_____

_____

_____

_____

_____

→ Why things did go well

_____

_____

_____

_____

_____

Why the outcomes were different

Think now about your responses to the two previous exercises.

→ Draw out the differences in how you felt, how you *perceived* things and the circumstances prevailing in the two situations.

_____

_____

_____

_____

_____

_____

_____

➜What does this tell you about your achievement
  orientation?

_____

_____

_____

➜What will you do?

_____

_____

_____

➜ Your life script

Who we are and how we behave is rooted in our
upbringing. It was the psychiatrist Eric Berne who suggested
that each of us has written our own life story, the pattern
by which we will live our lives. We begin 'writing' it at
birth through associating feelings with particular events

in our lives. By three or four years old, we have decided on the broad storyline. Some three or four years later we have fleshed out the plot. As we go through life, we use our continuing experiences of growing up to add colour and flavour to the script so that, by our teenage years, we have a fully scripted play with all the characters we need to enable us to live out the story.

In their book *TA Today: A New Introduction to Transactional Analysis*, Stewart and Joines tell us, 'Now that you are an adult, the beginnings of your story are out of reach of your conscious memory'. They go on to say that we probably did not even know that we had such a story. Yet we live it out on a daily basis because it is our life script. It has the following characteristics:

▶ it is directed towards a payoff
▶ it is decisional
▶ it is reinforced by parents
▶ it is outside of awareness
▶ it involves a redefinition of reality to justify the script
▶ it is about survival.

Your script has both content ('what') and process ('how'). It can be a *winning script* in which someone accomplishes a declared purpose, a *losing script* in which someone does not achieve a declared purpose, or a *non-winning script* in which someone drifts along from day to day, making neither significant wins nor losses.

It is important to recognize that by bringing your life script into consciousness, you can change it; you are not stuck with it. You can rewrite your script to reflect the new ending you wish to create in your play. You can do this is by applying high EQ to your life.

Your life script

Important: If this exercise brings back too many painful memories or you find it too emotionally challenging, STOP. Leave the exercise and carry on with the rest of this chapter.

Sit quietly on your own and think about your life script. Think about how your parents brought you up, and how your brothers and sisters, your friends and relations treated you. As you grew up, did the way any of them treated you change for the better or worse? What about your authority figures at school and elsewhere? So what script did you write about how you would live your life? Was it a winning script or a losing script? How does it come to an end? What is its title?

Now record your thinking in the box below.

→ Life-script title

_____

_____

→ Kind of story

_____

_____

_____

_____

→ Closing scene

_____

_____

_____

_____

→ How do you feel today about that life script?

_____

_____

_____

_____

_____

_____

→ Do you want change it in any way? How, and for what purpose?

_____

_____

_____

_____

_____

_____

The purpose of this exercise is to highlight that most of us live our lives according to our life script but we don't have to. You can choose to change your script simply by acknowledging how it is now and rewriting the play, including new actors who have a positive influence in your life and bringing the script to a close in a positive and energizing ending. Draw on all of the emotional intelligence competencies you have developed to change your way of being. Lead your life the way *you* choose.

Summary

In this chapter we looked at achievement orientation and what it is, including the behaviours of:

▶ being results-oriented, with a high drive to meet objectives and standards

▶ setting challenging goals and taking calculated risks

▶ pursuing information to reduce uncertainty and finding ways to do better

▶ learning how to improve performance.

We also saw why it's important, looking particularly at how the way you have lived your life up to now has affected your drive to succeed. You have had the opportunity to change your life script to a more positive and energizing way of being, significantly enhancing your achievement orientation.

12 Organizational awareness

In this chapter we look at organizational awareness, what it is and why it is important. Office politics is a major part of organizational awareness and we also explore the positive and negative aspects of office politics. We also spend time looking at position and personal power bases.

You will do exercises to improve your understanding of the subject and rehearse the skills required.

WHAT IT IS

'Hard work is rewarding. Taking credit for other people's hard work is also rewarding ... and faster.'

Unknown

Organizational awareness involves:

▶ knowing the organization's mission and functions

▶ knowing how its political, social and technological systems work

▶ operating effectively within its systems, including the programmes, policies, procedures, rules, and regulations of the organization.

Within these systems, it's the political system – the office politics – that is the exciting and frequently ruthless part. While the rules, regulations and procedures are usually well-documented, understood and generally complied with, office politics are not documented and operate at overt and covert levels. There are rules but not everyone operates to the same rules. So organizational awareness can be about survival.

→ Why organizational awareness is important

For your survival within your organization, it's important to:

▶ be fully conversant with your organization's ways of being and ways of operating

▶ identify the real decision-makers within your organization and who their allies, supporters and champions are; these are where the power lies

▶ understand how the dynamics of today's seemingly constant change might affect your position within the organization

▶ be prepared for the impact that today's seemingly constant change can have on others and how they might react.

You can be one of the people within your organization who lets things happen or one who makes things happen. The opportunities to make things happen might depend on your position within the hierarchy but the more you demonstrate the desire to make things happen, the more opportunity you are likely to be given. Fully integrating yourself into the organization's ways of being and ways of operating means that you have to acknowledge the power systems and use them appropriately.

→ Office politics

There can be few of us who have not, at some stage in our careers, encountered office politics. Indeed some of us might be so bold as to suggest that there is no such beast as an organization in which office politics does not form a substantial part of the culture. Wherever people are assembled together, office politics will emerge sooner or later; it's a natural phenomenon of human behaviour.

'Office politics is the use of one's individual or assigned power within an employing organization for the purpose of obtaining advantages beyond one's legitimate authority. Those advantages may include access to tangible assets, or intangible benefits such as status or pseudo-authority that influences the behaviour of others. Both individuals and groups may engage in office politics.'

Marilyn Haight

An important feature of this definition is the suggestion that office politics can exist at both individual and group levels. You can probably think of an individual in your own organization whom you recognize as a player of office politics. When it comes to group office politics, the frequent juxtaposition of management and unions is an excellent illustration.

THE NATURE OF OFFICE POLITICS

Office politics is not new. It has been around ever since people have worked together. Why? Because we are individuals with different personalities, different values, different opinions, different aspirations and different backgrounds who are all thrown in together.

What perhaps makes office politics more prevalent today is that we invariably operate in an environment where high performance and greater achievement, promotion and personal development are seen as essential elements of organizational and personal success. So in order to stand out from the crowd, you may play games which are designed to give you some advantage over your peers.

Think of yourself in a modern, progressive organization where leadership is about empowering people to be creative and innovative; where the vision is shared by everyone, at all levels; where people bring all of themselves to the workplace because they are fully engaged with what the organization is doing. What would office politics look and feel like there? They will probably still exist, but the chances are that they will be much less aggressive and disruptive; they will be more positive than negative; they will be more overt.

Office politics in your organization

Think of your current or a recent workplace. In the boxes below, create an influence chart for your organization and compare it to the organization's formal structure.

Influence chart	Formal structure

What does this reveal about the working of the organization?

_____

_____

_____

_____

POSITIVE AND NEGATIVE OFFICE POLITICS

Office politics is often regarded as a culture where games are played to gain individual advantage. This suggests that office politics is essentially negative but there are also positive office-politics strategies that can be deployed to the advantage of both individuals and the organization itself.

Positive office politics may be achieved through the following behaviours.

▶ **Genuinely care.** Showing genuine care and concern for others is very quickly noticed; equally, acting the part is picked up on rapidly and is hugely damaging to your reputation.

▶ **Develop relationships.** Actively notice the working relationships that successful people within the organization have with colleagues and what the characteristics of these are. Build your own relationships at all levels, but especially with influential people who will be advocates of you personally and of your organizational goals.

▶ **Share knowledge.** Make your knowledge available to others. Being seen as a trusted source of information means that people will beat a path to your door, which in turn will raise your personal profile.

▶ **Be approachable.** Being approachable for help and advice beyond the realm of your knowledge also raises your profile and augments your relationship-building strategies.

▶ **Be visible.** You need to be visible and observable. Others will see that you are popular, they'll see that you operate in a helpful and professional way and they'll recognize your commitment.

▶ **Get a mentor.** Having a mentor can be like having access to an 'inner circle'. Not only do you gain from different, possibly greater, experience, but you are also building relationships, undertaking self-development and demonstrating commitment.

Negative office politics are characterized by the following behaviours and impacts.

▶ **Gossiping.** It's natural for there to be a good deal of gossip around the office. It's usually better not to contribute to the gossip and, if possible, to remain somewhat removed from it as you can become embroiled by association.

▶ **Back-stabbing.** Back-stabbing is particularly underhanded as those who indulge in it will appear to be supportive of you while actually undermining you, perhaps because you are perceived as being in the way, e.g. a competitor for promotion. This is about them attempting to look good at your expense.

▶ **Blame transfer.** This is a specific form of back-stabbing. Some people are adept at transferring blame from themselves to others involved in an issue. It may be undertaken by inference rather than by directly pointing the finger. Such people are characterized by showing a general lack of responsibility.

▶ **Bullying.** The bully in the workplace generally has some power over the victim, e.g. they may be in a superior position, may have some information about you that they can use against you, or they may be physically or mentally aggressive. Bullies usually have an inferiority complex about a characteristic that they feel they must mask. Find the characteristic and you can remove the mask.

▶ **Passing the buck.** Passing the buck can simply be a denial of responsibility or capability. It's often employed by superiors when they don't want the responsibility. Passing the buck is different from the legitimate practice of delegation.

▶ **The ideas thief.** Some people find it difficult to shine beside others so when a good idea comes to light, they jump in to grab the glory. In 'broad daylight' the theft will be obvious; equally, it may happen under wraps and out of earshot so that finding out about it is more difficult and recovery is seriously impaired.

▶ **An unsupportive line manager.** You need to get along with your line manager for the obvious reason that they have considerable control over your destiny. You don't have to like them but hopefully can achieve a position of mutual respect that will make the relationship workable. This can be a difficult problem to tackle, but a diplomatic and mature approach will generally bring any issue out into the open so that it can be dealt with.

My use of office politics

In the boxes below, list some of the positive and negative office politics strategies you have used. Describe the effects they had (short-term and long-term) and how you felt about applying them.

Positive strategies	Effects	How I felt
1		
2		
3		
4		

Negative strategies	Effects	How I felt
1		
2		
3		
4		

→ Power bases

Understanding power bases is an important aspect of organizational awareness. Power exists within two distinct frames: position power and personal power.

POSITION POWER

This type of power derives from a person's position in a hierarchy or formal structure. It is recognized and largely accepted by people because they are aware of the organizational structure and its relative 'rankings'. Therefore, this power base can be applied to staff but not to your bosses.

Dr Frank Petrock suggests that position power breaks down into:

▶ legitimate power
▶ reward power
▶ coercive power.

Legitimate power is the type of position power most closely linked to position in a hierarchy. Your power derives from your position and title, which give you authority over others and a 'right to manage'. You can get by on just this power but it is based on a 'push' rather than a 'pull' philosophy. It does not earn you points in the popularity stakes. It can be seen as being both positive and negative, depending upon the manner of its use and the perceptions of the receiver.

Reward power is about providing incentives that people want and value, such as salary, recognition, bonus systems, promotions, etc. It's the 'carrot' that makes you go to work each day and makes you try to improve. Not all of us are inspired by the same rewards, so a 'one size fits all' approach is not going to be universally accepted.

Coercive power is the power to threaten punitive retaliation for 'misdemeanours'; these may be formal or sometimes informal sanctions against bad, unwanted or inappropriate behaviour. It can take many forms including a poor performance appraisal, a reprimand, criticism, demotion, suspension and, ultimately, dismissal. The process under which it is administered must be universally understood and rigorously applied.

PERSONAL POWER

Personal power has its origins within you, as part of who you are. It has much less to do with a job role or position within a hierarchy and much more to do with earned respect. Personal power makes you much more powerful in terms of winning people over and engendering engagement and buy-in than any position power basis.

Dr Petrock suggests that there are four types of personal power:

► connection power
► information power
► expert power
► referent power.

Connection power is about the connections you have with other influential and powerful people. They will be part of your network, and your relationship with them is seen as adding to your own power and influence. Of course, your connections must be perceived as being of value.

Information power is about your access to information that other people don't have, perhaps because access is restricted or because they don't know it exists. People have to know that you have privileged access to important and relevant information.

Expert power is based upon your expertise in a particular area that is important to the organization and not readily available from other internal sources. It can derive from experience, skill, knowledge and reputation. People are likely to come to you for advice and assistance because they trust your expertise.

Referent power is about how attractive you appear to others. This is about charisma, that aura which others pick up on and want to be associated with. So they'll expect you to step in where others are more reluctant, to lead where others stand back. They hang on to your coat-tails because they trust that you will sort things out and they may benefit from being a part of your solution. As Petrock says, 'Referent power is truly in the "eye of the beholder".'

If you have neither position power nor personal power, your choices in life are limited. If you have position power without personal power, then you are only able to get what you want in areas where your position has influence. However, if you have personal power, then you are able to influence and inspire people regardless of your position. It's best to have both forms of power but to use your personal power in preference to your position power.

Observations of power use

Think about two very different people you have encountered in a work situation, one you admired and another who impressed you rather less. Think about the power they wielded. Try to rank by frequency of use each of the three position power bases and four personal power bases they deployed and why; did they have a preference for one power over others? What were the circumstances when their use of power was appropriate or inappropriate, and what was the overall impact on you?

Use the following table to record your thinking. Where you have no evidence of a power base being used, leave the row blank.

Person A (admired)

Power base	Frequency of use	Circumstances (why?)	Appropriate/ Inappropriate	Impact on you (positive/ negative)
Position power				
Legitimate				
Reward				
Coercive				
Personal power				
Connection				
Information				
Expert				
Referent				

Person B (less admired)

Power base	Frequency of use	Circumstances (why?)	Appropriate/ Inappropriate	Impact on you (positive/ negative)
Position power				
Legitimate				
Reward				
Coercive				
Personal power				
Connection				
Information				
Expert				
Referent				

Make notes below to explain the differences in behaviour between the two people.

→ The differences

_____

_____

_____

_____

_____

_____

→ What this tells me

_____

_____

_____

_____

_____

_____

My use of power

Turning to your own use of power, repeat the above exercise with regard to your own use of power and its impact on others. For this exercise to be of value, you need to be honest about yourself. If possible, get a

close colleague to complete the exercise about you, or at the least involve that person in the process.

My use of power

Power base	Frequency of use	Circumstances (why?)	Appropriate/ Inappropriate	Impact on you (positive/ negative)
Position power				
Legitimate				
Reward				
Coercive				
Personal power				
Connection				
Information				
Expert				
Referent				

Record below observations about your own use of power, i.e. its implications, how you feel about yourself and your take on how others might view your use of power.

My use of power

→ Implications of my use of power

_____

_____

_____

_____

_____

_____

_____

→ How I feel about myself

_____

_____

_____

_____

_____

_____

_____

_____

→How I think others felt

_____

_____

_____

_____

_____

_____

Summary

This chapter looked at organizational awareness, what it is and how to engage with it. We looked at the nature of office politics, including:

▶ positive office politics: genuinely care, develop relationships, share knowledge, be approachable, be visible, get a mentor

▶ negative office politics: gossiping, back-stabbing, blame transfer, bullying, passing the buck, the ideas thief, an unsupportive line manager.

We also looked at power bases: position power, consisting of legitimate power, reward power and coercive power; and personal power, consisting of connection power; information power, expert power and referent power.

13 *Teamwork and collaboration*

This chapter is about teamwork and collaboration. We look at what it is and why it is important to you. Then we examine the nature of both teamwork and collaboration and what the essential competencies are.

You will do some exercises to establish your skills and any gaps that might exist, followed by more exercises to rehearse you in those skills.

WHAT IT IS

'None of us is as smart as all of us.'

Japanese proverb

In today's connected world, teamwork and collaboration are essential for organizational success. Ask yourself how much of the knowledge that you use at work resides in your own mind; you are probably reliant on having a network of people around you who know things that you need in addition to your own knowledge. It is a clearly established fact that organizations that are team-based enjoy greater success than those that are not. Of course, some teams are more successful than others and how that comes about could be the subject of a book in its own right; there is plenty of recent research into group working. Here, we're concerned with the basic skills that engender great teamwork and collaboration.

Daniel Goleman's *Working with Emotional Intelligence* and later works identified the respective competencies as follows:

Teamwork	Collaboration
What it is: *creating group synergy in pursuing collective goals*	***What it is:*** *working with others towards shared goals*
People with this competency: ▶ *model team qualities like respect, helpfulness and co-operation* ▶ *draw all members into active and enthusiastic participation* ▶ *build team identity and commitment* ▶ *protect the group and its reputation* ▶ *share the credit*	*People with this competency:* ▶ *balance a focus on the task with attention to relationships* ▶ *collaborate, sharing plans, information and resources* ▶ *promote a friendly, co-operative climate* ▶ *spot and nurture opportunities for collaboration*

When you think about working together as a team, there are two elements to what you must do. The first is the task you are undertaking; you may be involved in a specific project, e.g. to manage the introduction of a new product or service, or it may be a more everyday task, e.g. to help to manage the organization's finances; these are the 'business as usual' (BAU) elements. Then there is your management of and contribution to the team itself; this is what you are concerned with in this chapter.

→ Why teamwork and collaboration are important

Teamwork and collaboration are key competencies that are usually looked for in recruitment today, so these competencies are important in your search for employment. They are also likely to be essential to your continued employment, since being a valued team member could well be an element of your competency framework (if you have one) and therefore part of your performance appraisal.

So teamwork and collaboration are vital to:

► employability
► career success
► self-esteem
► personal well-being.

My teamwork skills questionnaire

Complete the self-assessment below. Against each of the competencies, tick a single response to each statement according to how frequently you show that behaviour; 'Never' scores 0 and 'Always' scores 4. Then add up your column scores to give your total score.

Grade	Legend and scoring instructions	Score
Always	There are no exceptions; you would have to think consciously about behaving any other way and changing what you do.	Add 4 points for every tick
Routinely	You would present yourself this way or react this way every week, with few exceptions.	Add 3 points for every tick
Some-times	At your best, this is what you would be seen doing.	Add 2 points for every tick
Rarely	It would be considered unusual for this to be what you say, think or do.	Add 1 point for every tick
Never	There would be no exceptions; you do not present yourself this way to people at any time.	No points

Statement	Never (0)	Rarely (1)	Sometimes (2)	Routinely (3)	Always (4)
I model team qualities like respect, helpfulness and co-operation					
I draw all members into active and enthusiastic participation					
I build team identity and commitment					
I protect the group and its reputation					
I share credit					
Column scores					
Total score					

Now check the feedback for your score.

Score = 13–16. Congratulations. You have well-developed teamworking skills which should stand you in good stead in your career.

Actions to take: With well-developed teamworking skills, you may choose to help others in your circle of influence. Doing so will benefit them and you will also gain from the interactions.

Score = 9–12. Well done, you should be pleased with the results. You would benefit from further developing your teamworking skills to maximize the success you clearly want to achieve.

Actions to take: Complete this chapter, especially the exercises it contains. You could also seek out someone you admire for their teamworking skills and ask for their support in improving your own.

Score = 5–8. Well done for completing this exercise. You can certainly take action to improve your teamworking skills if you choose to do so. Some people's roles do not emphasize working collectively and are more stand-alone. If you do not need to prioritize this capability for working with others or other community/family projects, then leave improvement of your score out of your personal development plan.

Actions to take: Complete this chapter, especially the exercises it contains. You could also seek out someone you admire for their teamworking skills and ask for their support in improving your own. Discuss the workflow in the role you are in and identify your contribution and that of those on whom you rely. In addition, you may wish to embark on a personal development course or a one-to-one coaching programme that would help you to explore any underlying issues to improve your teamworking skills and, ultimately, your personal success.

Score = 0–4. Thank you for being so honest. Showing integrity is a great emotional intelligence strength. Remind yourself how much of the knowledge that you use at work resides in your own mind; you are probably reliant on having a network of people around you who know things that you need in addition to your own knowledge. Consider and discuss with your trusted adviser what you can do to improve your teamworking; doing so is likely to bring greater success in both your personal and working lives.

Actions to take: You may decide that pursuing this skill further is not a priority. However, you would benefit greatly from completing this chapter and perhaps revisiting previous chapters, as this book has been gradually building your skills towards achieving greater success in your life. In addition, you may wish to embark on a personal development course or a one-to-one coaching programme that would help you to improve your teamworking skills and, ultimately, your personal success.

My collaboration skills questionnaire

Complete the self-assessment below. Against each of the competencies, tick a single response to each statement according to how frequently you show that behaviour; 'Never' scores 0 and 'Always' scores 4. Then add up your column scores to give your total score.

Grade	Legend and scoring instructions	Score
Always	There are no exceptions; you would have to think consciously about behaving any other way and changing what you do.	Add 4 points for every tick
Routinely	You would present yourself this way or react this way every week, with few exceptions.	Add 3 points for every tick
Sometimes	At your best, this is what you would be seen doing.	Add 2 points for every tick
Rarely	It would be considered unusual for this to be what you say, think or do.	Add 1 point for every tick
Never	There would be no exceptions; you do not present yourself this way to people at any time.	No points

Statement	Never (0)	Rarely (1)	Sometimes (2)	Routinely (3)	Always (4)
I balance a focus on the task with attention to relationships					
I collaborate, sharing plans, information and resources					
I promote a friendly, co-operative climate					
I spot and nurture opportunities for collaboration					
Column scores					
Total score					

Now check the feedback for your score.

Score = 13–16. Congratulations. You have high to exceptional collaboration skills, which should enable you to work extremely well in teamworking situations and in developing relationships.

Actions to take: With well-developed collaboration skills, you may choose to help others in your circle of influence. Doing so will benefit them and you will also gain from the interactions.

Score = 9–12. Well done, you should be pleased with the results. You would benefit from further developing your collaboration skills to maximize the success you clearly want to achieve.

Actions to take: Complete this chapter, especially the exercises it contains. You could also seek out someone you admire for their collaboration skills and ask for their support in improving your own. Think about the common processes and goals on which you work with others.

Score = 5–8. Well done for completing this exercise. You can certainly take action to improve your collaboration skills if you choose to do so. Check out the expectations and assumptions of members in the team of each other.

Actions to take: Complete this chapter, especially the exercises it contains. You could also seek out someone you admire for their collaboration skills and ask for their support in improving your own; discuss plenty of examples relevant to your roles of co-operation and collaboration so that you feel the need and pertinence of personal development here. In addition, you may wish to embark on a personal development course or a coaching programme which would help you to improve your collaboration skills and, ultimately, your personal success.

Score = 0–4. Thank you for being so honest. Showing integrity is a great emotional intelligence strength. You can do much to improve your collaboration skills, and doing so is likely to bring greater success in both your personal and working lives. Think about the relationships, common processes and goals on which you work with others. Pick out insights and plan actions for improvement.

Actions to take: If you are happy with your current levels of success, then you may decide that you do not wish to pursue this skill further. However, you would benefit greatly from completing this chapter and perhaps revisiting previous chapters as this book has been gradually building your skills towards achieving greater success in your life. In addition, you may wish to embark on a personal development course or a coaching programme which would help you to improve your collaboration skills and, ultimately, your personal success.

Thus far you have looked at your personal involvement in your team. Now you should consider the team-wide factors which affect its effectiveness and how you can develop greater achievement orientation.

→ Beckhard's model of team effectiveness

Richard Beckhard's research into team effectiveness resulted in outcomes suggesting that teams have to manage four internal aspects of the way they work together. These are:

▶ goal-setting

▶ roles

▶ processes

▶ relationships.

Subsequently, a further factor was added: how the team manages its interaction within the organizational and external environment.

Based on Beckhard's model of team effectiveness

The organizational and external environment is the climate and culture within which the team operates. It is influenced by external factors, such as industry sector, regulatory regime and geographic dispersal, and by internal factors like organizational structure, leadership styles, etc. So this aspect concerns the impact of the organization and the outside world on team behaviour.

GOAL-SETTING

Teamwork is about achieving common goals. So it is important that goals are:

▶ clear to all
▶ understood by all
▶ communicated to all
▶ owned/shared by all
▶ congruent with everyone in the team.

Explore the degree of ownership of team goals, as low levels of ownership often result in the common pitfalls of unassigned tasks, mismatched expectations and conflict. Check:

▶ the extent to which goals are defined, quantified and deliverable
▶ the extent to which goals are shared or congruent
▶ the extent of goal conflict or divergence.

Signs to look for: The goals are unclear or not communicated, everyone is doing their own thing, team members are not participating in goal-setting, or gaps in task allocation are known but tasks remain unassigned.

ROLES

Check who does what on the team, and explore the following issues:

▶ do all members understand what they and others are to do to accomplish the task? A responsibility assignment matrix (RACI) chart is essential, whether the work is a normal operation or a special project.

▶ do they know their individual responsibilities and limits of authority? Terms of reference that include delegated limits of authority, liaison relationships and functional reporting lines really help.

In new teams, time should be spent discussing and defining roles and responsibilities; this is particularly important in projects where there are milestones and delivery dates to meet. As the team develops, it is typical for individuals to build expectations and assumptions of others which are seldom recorded anywhere; tasks assigned at group level do not get done – there needs to be a name in the frame.

In projects, there is a life cycle that changes the focus of work from one phase to another, as different specialists' skills are required and then rolled off the project. Responsibilities and boundaries should be discussed, agreed upon and promulgated. Modern technology makes it easy to inform team members of new joiners and responsibility changes.

Conflict may occur because of differing expectations among team members, overlaps, omissions, different contexts, etc. Overlapping roles can create conflict, especially when two or more team members see themselves as the expert on-site and responsible for the same tasks; boundaries must be established in scope, context, time frames or other delineation.

Signs to look for: Responsibilities are poorly defined, there is a power vacuum, members act independently and avoid responsibility. The reporting structure will begin to see duplication as reports are filed month on month; equally, gaps may emerge near delivery dates.

PROCESSES

Once team members know what they are to do and who is to do it, they must determine how they will work together.

The RACI chart helps with workflow as well as delineating responsibility levels. Typical considerations are:

▶ decision-making – how will each of the team members participate in decision-making?

▶ communication – what messages should be communicated within the team, to whom, by what method, how much, when and how frequently?

▶ meetings – what is the team trying to achieve (customer delivery, internal milestones), what are the agenda items to be covered, who is responsible for each item, was there preparatory work and how will the meeting be conducted, who should attend?

▶ management style – the leader and the team agree the most appropriate style to meet the situation and the leader should be open to receiving feedback from the team.

Signs to look for: Meetings are unproductive or poorly attended, decision-making is dominated by one or two people, actions are taken without planning, communication is one way, any action points are not summarized at the end of discussions so there is no productive outcome.

RELATIONSHIPS

The quality of interaction among team members can often suffer as team members work together, with relationships becoming strained. Individual members must have ways of resolving issues to ensure good working relationships continue. Sometimes relationship problems occur because of a difference in values or a personality or management-style clash. Managers may need to take an active role in soothing relationships during times of conflict. The more energy that is diverted by bad feelings, poor attitudes or strong emotions, the less energy there is available for the team's task.

Signs to look for: There are personality conflicts, team members are defensive or competitive.

→ Team development

Team development is a process intended to improve team performance in any one or all of the five factors in team effectiveness: goal-setting; roles; processes; relationships; the organizational and external environment. After examining your team's performance in these areas, your role as a manager is to identify where your focus for team development needs to be.

My team development

We have encouraged you to develop a personal development plan. Identify what you need to add to your personal development plan to start demonstrating greater ability to work with others:

► the things that you do that breach trust or break teamwork and collaboration with employees and other colleagues
► the things that you need to do more or less often in order to be more collaborative
► what is the cost of being weak at teamwork?

Development needs

1 _____

_____

_____

_____

2 _____

_____

_____

_____

3 _____

_____

_____

_____

4 _____

_____

_____

_____

5 _____

_____

_____

_____

Clearly, poor teamwork and collaboration outcomes are best avoided by raising your EQ. Summarize your development needs and potential outcomes of any low EQ habits and plan the actions in your personal development plan that you need to:

▶ start doing

▶ stop doing

▶ do more often

▶ do less often.

Your PDP action plan	
I will start ...	*I will do more ...*
I will stop ...	*I will do less ...*

Summary

For teams to be effective they must manage four areas internal to the team: goals, roles, processes and relationships. The EQ competencies in teamwork and collaboration should be seen as high a priority for most people's roles as their technical skills and knowledge; it is rare to truly work alone.

References and resources

All URLs were active as at May 2012.

HOW TO USE THIS WORKBOOK

For a definition of IQ and Binet's work, see: http://hiqnews.megafoundation.org/Definition_of_IQ1.html

An independent overview of assessments, commentary by practitioners, example frameworks and client case studies are contained in:

Dann, J., *Instant Manager: Emotional Intelligence* (Hodder Education, 2008)

Dann, J., *Teach Yourself: Emotional Intelligence In A Week* (Teach Yourself, 2012)

CHAPTER 1

Honey, P., http://www.peterhoney.com (2009)

Houle, C. O., *Continuing learning in the professions* (Jossey-Bass, 1980)

Knowles, M., *Self-directed Learning: A guide for learners and teachers* (Prentice Hall, 1975)

Smith, M. K. 'David A. Kolb on experiential learning' (2001), *The encyclopedia of informal education* at http://www.infed.org/biblio/b-explrn.htm

On Kolb's learning cycle and learning styles inventory: http://www.businessballs.com/kolblearningstyles.htm

On Honey and Mumford's learning styles: http://www.peterhoney.com/

On wisdom and knowledge: http://www.davemckay.co.uk/philosophy/russell/russell.php?name=knowledge.and.wisdom

Honey, P., 'Action plans – what a struggle!' at http://www.peterhoney.com/documents/HowGoodAreActionplans-pressrelease14Jan10.pdf

CHAPTER 2

Henry, J. P. and Stephens, P. M., *Stress, Health and the Social Environment: A sociobiologic approach to medicine* (Springer Verlag, 1977)

'The brain from top to bottom' at http://thebrain.mcgill.ca/flash/i/i_04/i_04_cl/i_04_cl_peu/i_04_cl_peu.html

Brain research as a help to pedagogy and best practice for teachers: Wilmes, B., Harrington, L., Kohler-Evans, P. and Sumpter, D., 'Coming to our senses: incorporating brain research findings into classroom instruction' (2008) at http://www.highbeam.com/doc/1G1-180277951.html

The stress hormone cortisol and its effects: eHow.com, 'What Are the Benefits of Cortisol?' (2011) http://www.ehow.com/list_6851540_benefits-cortisol_.html#ixzz1nJNcN6w3

Perhaps the most dominant figure in advancing left brain/right brain concepts in education was Joseph Bogen MD of Caltech (http://www.its.caltech.edu/~jbogen), who, along with R. Sperry and H. G. Gordon, conducted the first split-brain study. It was Bogen's view that society had overemphasized propositionality (left-hemisphere dominance in speaking, writing and calculations) at the expense of appositionality (right-hemisphere dominance in intuitive, creative and spatial matters). Bogen believed that such a focus on the left hemisphere was driven by society's belief that left-hemisphere activities most readily predicted success for society. He argued that 'such measures are very narrow and do not take into account artistic creativity and other right-hemisphere skills that are not easily quantifiable' (Springer/Deutsch 298).

The idea that our educational system favours one-half of our mental capability at the expense of the other has been appearing with increasing frequency in educational journals and self-help manuals. Concepts for education have become about what education can do to augment left-hemisphere development by helping to develop the underdeveloped right-hemisphere focus on creativity, complex relationships and spatial patterns.

http://www.sciencemag.org/content/early/2011/07/13/science.1207745

Brain damage rarely affects just one of these systems. Rather, the disruptive effects of most brain injuries, regardless of their size or location, usually involve all three systems:

Lezak, M. D., *Neuropsychological Assessment* (2nd ed.) (OUP, 1983)

The effects of brain damage on the functioning of the brain, especially with regard to decision-making: http://neurophilosophy.wordpress.com/2007/03/22/a-neural-substrate-for-moral-decisions/ and http://www.nytimes.com/2007/03/22/science/22brain.html?_r=1&ref=science&oref=slogin

Podcast interview with Marc Hauser (2007): http://neurophilosophy.wordpress.com/2007/03/08/podcast-interview-with-marc-hauser/

The incredible case of Phineas Gage (2006): http://neurophilosophy.wordpress.com/2006/12/04/the-incredible-case-of-phineas-gage/

CHAPTER 4

The BBC has a self-control questionnaire at: http://www.bbc.co.uk/science/humanbody/mind/surveys/selfcontrol/

The *Psychology Today* e-zine has a great deal of information at: http://www.psychologytoday.com/basics/self-control

WikiHow has a piece on how to develop self-control at: http://www.wikihow.com/Build-Self-Control

CHAPTER 5

Restall, L., 'In pursuit of excellence, overcoming under-achievement: Effective strategies for teachers', Overcoming Under-achievement seminar

Abraham Maslow (1908–70) developed the hierarchy of needs model in the USA in the 1940–50s, and the hierarchy of needs theory remains valid today for understanding human motivation, management training and personal development.

CHAPTER 6

If you are working or interested in being 'aware of others' in a more global sense, see Fons Trompenaars' work on cross-cultural competencies, which covers development for diversity, cultural awareness, innovation and leadership to improve transcultural communication based on mutual understanding of different cultural norms. See: http://www.thtconsulting.com/Website/AboutTHT/Bios/FT.asp

Empathy

There are some excellent books and articles that help individuals recognize empathy and how it positively impacts on performance. Some provide explicit descriptions of the behaviours associated with the competency; some describe the impact of the presence or absence of empathy; and others provide research about what it is and why it is important:

▶ Heyman, R, *Why Didn't You Say That in the First Place? How to Be Understood at Work* (Jossey-Bass, 1994). This book gives information on how to communicate effectively and avoid misunderstandings; it also discusses how to make sense of what other people say.

▶ Rogers, C. R., *Client-Centered Therapy: Its Current Practice Implications and Theory* (Houghton Mifflin, 1951)

▶ Swets, P. W., *The Art of Talking so that People Will Listen: Getting Through to Family, Friends, and Associates* (Prentice Hall, 1983)

Films and television programmes lending themselves to analysis of empathy include:

▶ *The Awakening*. This film shows how paying close attention to what people do can lead to deep empathy. The film is particularly appropriate for this competency since most of the clues observed are nonverbal.

▶ *The Inn of the Sixth Happiness.* Ingrid Bergman shows unusual empathy and strength in responding to a totally foreign situation. The film also shows how the competency develops out of an intense concern for and caring for others.

▶ *Call the Midwife.* This BBC TV series shows many examples of empathy between medical professionals and expectant mothers.

Service orientation

Books and articles helping individuals understand what service orientation looks like and how it positively impacts on performance include:

▶ Albrecht, K. and Zemke, R., *Service America: Doing Business in the New Economy* (Warner Books, 1995 reprint)

▶ Bell, C. R., *Customers as Partners: Building Relationships That Last* (Berrett-Koehler, 1994)

▶ Johnston, R., 'A framework for developing a quality strategy in a customer processing operation' (1987), *International Journal of Quality and Reliability*, Vol. 4 No. 4, p35–44

▶ Peters, T., *Thriving on Chaos* (Knopf, 1988) This groundbreaking book discusses aspects of managing chaos gained from experience at seminars.

▶ Sewell, C. and Brown, P. B., *Customers for Life: How to Turn the One-Time Buyer into a Lifetime Customer* (Doubleday Currency, 1991)

▶ Whiteley, R. C. *The Customer Driven Company: Moving from Talk to Action* (Perseus, 1991)

Films providing good illustrations of the presence or absence of service orientation include:

▶ *But I Don't Have Customers: Internal Customer Service*, AMI, AHS Videos

- *Customer-Driven Service*, American Management Association
- *Customer Service: It's Everyone's Job*, American Management Association
- *Moments of Truth*, Albrecht, AHS Videos
- *Service Excellence*, Video Arts. This film examines how Jan Carlson made Scandinavian Airlines into an industry leader through customer service. It is a good guide for thinking about customer focus.

CHAPTER 7

Goffee, R. and Jones, G., *Why Should Anyone Be Led by You* (Harvard Business School Press, 2006)

Truss, K., Soane, E. et al, *Working Life: Employee Engagement and Attitudes* (CIPD, 2006)

Developing others

Useful books include:
- Byham, W. and Cox, J., *Zapp!: Lightning of Empowerment* (Random House, 1991)
- Fournies, F., *Coaching for Improved Work Performance* (F. Fournies & Associates, 1987)
- Kinlaw, D. C., *Coaching for Commitment* (Jossey-Bass, 1999)
- Kolb, D., *Experiential Learning* (FT/Prentice Hall, 1983)
- Mink, O., Owen, K., Mink, B., *Developing High Performance People* (Basic Books, 1993)

Films offering case analyses include:
- *Chariots of Fire*. This film about training for the Olympics has numerous scenes of coaching and development, focusing on the person rather than just the task.

- *Good Will Hunting.* This depicts someone being brought to see his opportunities in the future, which empowers him to overcome maltreatment and triumph in adverse conditions.
- *The Karate Kid.* This story of an adolescent who learns how to fight and how not to fight has a good depiction of empowerment along with development.

Inspirational leadership

Useful books include:

- Conner, D., *Leading at the Edge of Chaos* (Wiley, 1998)
- Covey, S., *Principle-centered Leadership* (Simon & Schuster, 1992)
- Crosby, P., *The Absolutes of Leadership* (Jossey-Bass, 1997)
- Hesselbein, F., Goldsmith, M. and Beckhard, R. (eds), *The Leader of the Future* (Jossey-Bass, 1996)
- Kouzes, J. M. and Posner, B. Z., *The Leadership Challenge Planner: An Action Guide to Achieving Your Personal Best* (Jossey-Bass, 1999)
- Kouzes, J. M. and Posner, B. Z., *Leadership Challenge: How to Get Extraordinary Things Done in Organizations* (Jossey-Bass, 1987)
- Semler, R., *Transformational Leadership* (1997)

Films offering case analyses include:

- *Henry V.* This is one of Shakespeare's many plays about leadership. Note especially the St Crispin's Day speech, a model for inspirational speeches.
- *Twelve O'Clock High.* This is an in-depth study of leadership: how it can fail and how it can succeed.

Change catalyst

Useful books include:

▶ Conner, D. *Managing at the Speed of Change: How Resilient Managers Succeed and Prosper Where Others Fail* (Random House, 1993)

▶ Hutton, D. W., *Change Agents' Handbook: A Survival Guide for Quality Improvement Champions* (ASQ Quality Press, 1994)

▶ Kotter, J. P., *Force for Change: How Leadership Differs from Management* (Free Press, 1990)

▶ Kotter, J. P., 'Leading Change' (1996), *Harvard Business Review*

▶ Moss Kanter, R., Stein, B. and Jick, T. D., *The Challenge of Organizational Change: How Companies Experience It and Leaders Guide It* (Free Press, 1992)

▶ Moss Kanter, R., *The Change Masters* (Simon & Schuster, 1983)

CHAPTER 8

Coutu, Diane L., 'How Resilience Works' (May 2002), *Harvard Business Review*

Kübler-Ross, E., *On Death and Dying* (Macmillan (NY), 1969), in which she first discussed what is now known as the Kübler-Ross model.

The American Psychological Association was founded in 1892 and now has some 150,000 members and 54 divisions in subfields of psychology: http://www.apa.org/about/archives/index.aspx

The Management Advisory Service provides analysis, consultancy, facilitation, training and coaching services that transform corporate culture, enhance staff wellbeing and performance, and prevent work-related stress. See http://www.mas.org.uk/quest/analysis1.htm for their online resilience questionnaire.

The Hay Group (http://www.haygroup.com/uk/) is a global management consulting firm that works with leaders to transform strategy into reality. They develop talent, organize people to be more effective and motivate them to perform at their best. The group produces a resilience workbook to help people improve their resilience: http://www.haygroup.com/leadershipandtalentondemand/ourproducts/item_details.aspx?itemid=116&type=4&t=1

CHAPTER 10

Dann, J., *Instant Manager: Emotional Intelligence* (Hodder Education, 2008); see Chapter 10 for more information about emotional intelligence and conflict resolution

Learn more about the Thomas-Kilmann conflict mode instrument at: http://www.kilmann.com/conflict.html

CHAPTER 11

Haight, M., *Who's Afraid of the Big Bad Boss* (Infinity Publishing, 2005)

Stewart, I. and Joines, V., *TA Today: A New Introduction to Transactional Analysis* (Lifespace Publishing, 1987)

Learn more about Eric Berne at: http://www.ericberne.com/

Learn more about Daniel Goleman at: http://danielgoleman.info/topics/emotional-intelligence/

CHAPTER 12

Learn more about Petrock and his coaching of business leaders in leading and managing change at: http://frankpetrock.com and http://frankpetrock.com/static.php?page=static080625-20s0255

CHAPTER 13

Beckhard, R., 'Optimising Team Building Efforts' (*Journal of Contemporary Business*, Summer 1972)

Goleman, D., *Working with Emotional Intelligence* (Bloomsbury, 1998), and later works

Clarity on responsibility assignment using a RACI chart http://www.valuebasedmanagement.net/methods_raci.html

Dixon, R. and Gould, O., 'Adults telling and retelling stories collaboratively' in Baltes, P. and Staudinger, U., *Interactive Minds: life-span perspectives on the social foundation of cognition* (CUP, 1996)

Hill, G. W., 'Group versus individual performance; Are N + 1 heads better than one?' (1982), *Psychological Bulletin*, Vol. 91 (3)

Williams, W. and Sternberg, R., 'Group intelligence: Why some groups are better than others' (1988), *Intelligence*, Vol. 12 (4)

Index